Modernism versus Traditionalism

REACTING TO THE PAST is an award-winning series of immersive role-playing games that actively engage students in their own learning. Students assume the roles of historical characters and practice critical thinking, primary source analysis, and argument, both written and spoken. Reacting games are flexible enough to be used across the curriculum, from first-year general education classes and discussion sections of lecture classes to capstone experiences, intersession courses, and honors programs.

Reacting to the Past was originally developed under the auspices of Barnard College and is sustained by the Reacting Consortium of colleges and universities. The Consortium hosts a regular series of conferences and events to support faculty and administrators.

Note to instructors: Before beginning the game you must download the Gamemaster's Materials, including an instructor's guide containing a detailed schedule of class sessions, role sheets for students, and handouts.

To download this essential resource, visit https://reactingconsortium.org/games, click on the page for this title, then click "Instructors Guide."

Modernism versus Traditionalism

ART IN PARIS, 1888–1889

GRETCHEN K. MCKAY,

NICOLAS W. PROCTOR,

AND MICHAEL A. MARLAIS

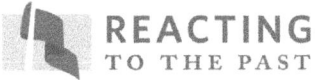

BARNARD

The University of North Carolina Press

Chapel Hill

The University of North Carolina Press has been a member of the
Green Press Initiative since 2003.

Cover illustration: Albumen silver print of the Eiffel Tower c. 1890.
(Photographer unknown; courtesy of the Metropolitan Museum of Art).

ISBN 978-1-4696-4126-3 (pbk.: alk. paper)
ISBN 978-1-4696-4127-0 (e-book)

Contents

Figures

PLEASE NOTE THE FOLLOWING WORKS OF ART THAT SHOULD BE EXAMINED VIA AN INTERNET SEARCH WHILE READING THIS GAMEBOOK.

You should find an image of the following paintings listed when they are mentioned in the text. You must LOOK at the image while you are reading and during the play of this reacting to the Past game. All images may not be reproduced in print due to copyright issues.

FOR PROLOGUE

Jean-Louis-Ernest Meissonier, *Friedland, 1807*, 1861–75
William-Adolphe Bouguereau, *Birth of Venus*, 1879
Claude Monet, *Impression, Sunrise*, 1872
Vincent Van Gogh, *Père Tanguy*, 1887
Pierre Puvis de Chavannes, *The Childhood of St. Geneviève*, 1876–78
Pierre Puvis de Chavannes, *The Poor Fisherman*, 1881
Georges Seurat, *Sunday Afternoon on the Island of La Grande Jatte*, 1884–86

FOR HISTORICAL NARRATIVE

Nicolas Poussin, *The Burial of Phocion*, 1648
Jean-Honoré Fragonard, *The Swing*, 1767
Jacques-Louis David, *Antiochus and Stratonice*, 1774
Gustave Courbet, *A Burial at Ornans*, 1850
Édouard Manet, *Déjeuner sur L'Herbe* (*Luncheon on the Grass*), 1862–63
Claude Monet, *Impression, Sunrise*, 1872
Édouard Detaille, *The Dream*, 1888

Modernism versus Traditionalism

1

Introduction

BRIEF OVERVIEW OF THE GAME

BRIEF OVERVIEW OF THE GAME

This is a "reacting" game. Reacting games use complex role-play to teach about particular moments in history. This game centers on art, specifically late nineteenth-century painting. In 1888, a wide diversity of art styles existed in Paris, which was the center of the art world.

While there were many different styles of painting, the Academy—established as the Royal Academy of Painting and Sculpture in 1648 by King Louis XIV—still held much power. The Academy was composed of fourteen members, elected for life. Academy members advocated realistically rendered scenes of uplifting mythological, biblical, and historical subjects, and showcased them at an annual Salon in central Paris.

Any artist could submit a work of art for the annual Salon. Thousands of paintings and sculptures were usually accepted, but many more were rejected, often due to loose brushstrokes or subject matter not considered morally uplifting. The same Academy members who accepted Salon entries then decided which works would be awarded prizes and medals.

The annual Salon was the most important art event of the year, and nearly every Parisian went to see the thousands of works displayed. Artists attended to see what types of art were being supported by the Academy and which pieces were worthy of prizes. Some artists agreed with the choices made, while others did not.

This game opens during the waning days of the 1888 Salon. Prizes have been given out. Édouard Detaille's painting *The Dream* has won a medal of honor and was one of the most celebrated paintings of the Salon. Much of the debate in the first session of the game will be about this painting and what this award means for the future of art.

The Impressionists are also painting in Paris. Although in 1888 they are no longer a cohesive group, having had their final group exhibition in 1886, there are many artists under this label still painting in the Impressionist manner, paying attention to light, color, and atmospheric conditions in the landscapes around them.

There are also the artists of the Avant-Garde. They abhor the Salon, the Academy, and all forms of traditional art. They are eager to try new things and are the first to explore and imagine new ways of expression. They include a group that critic Félix Fénéon refers to as the "Neo-Impressionists." These are artists who paint in a style that separates colors into different daubs of paint on the canvas.

Art in Paris offers a chance to view, describe, and debate the full range of artistic styles and movements in 1888 and 1889. In addition to artists, players include art critics, who seek to advance their preferred aesthetics, and art dealers, who focus on work that appeals to their customers. Their discussions and views about art culminate in the 1889 World's Fair held in Paris (the Exposition Universelle). All artists are required to show their works at the exposition—as part of the annual Salon, through a gallery show, with a group of like-minded artists, or even alone. There are many options, just as there are many artists and artistic styles.

PROLOGUE

It is 1888, and you are in Paris. You are an art lover. You have even been known to do a little sketching and have tried your hand at painting in the past. You are not an academically trained artist by any means, but you are interested, as are most Parisians, in the goings-on of the art world. Art has always been considered a national pastime. Indeed, throughout this century, art has been considered the pride of France.

Yet lately there have been some changes in the art world that are confusing. Traditional paintings that highlight the heroes of French history are still being created, but you have heard about painters who eschew such traditional subjects and paint modern views of the city of Paris. Some paint ordinary workers and scenes of everyday life—the mundane of our world. You wonder if art should elevate the common man or if it should evoke a

world beyond our current troubles by depicting noble subjects of France's past triumphs. Others proclaim that a new century is dawning and that art should be a herald of the newness to come. Some of these individuals support art that doesn't reflect nature at all, depicting lakes of red water and skies of green. What are some of these people doing? you wonder.

Because you are not sure what you think about these new ideas, you decide that you will devote the day to seeing art—in all its forms. There are so many styles of art in Paris, and today you will attempt to see as much as you can.

You start at the Musée de Luxembourg, for it is here that works of art from the previous Salons are displayed. As you walk down the halls, you are very moved by the works that highlight the triumphs of France. Meissonier's *Friedland, 1807*, painted in 1875, expertly captures the celebratory moment during the final phase of the battle of Friedland, when the emperor Napoleon and his staff reviewed the 12th Regiment of Cuirassiers as they charged past, victorious. Meissonier captured many details, and it is clear that he studied the regiment and wanted to be as accurate as possible.

You are also captivated by paintings with a more mythological focus. For instance, you can't seem to pull your eyes off of Bouguereau's *Birth of Venus* from 1879. You are mesmerized as Venus, the goddess of love and beauty, emerges from the sea. The depiction of classical nymphs, and the goddess herself, demonstrates Bouguereau's mastery of the human form.

After spending several hours at the Musée de Luxembourg, you decide to stop and view the images that are currently displayed at the Durand-Ruel Gallery. You have been here before and seen the works of Claude Monet. You appreciate the paintings, but you also wonder if showing poppies in a field or images of rivers and bridges provides a foundation for high art. You are not sure. Yet clearly these works have an interesting color scheme. Their compositions fascinate you, and the way the artists have applied the paint is very different from what you observed at the Musée de Luxembourg. In those paintings—by Meissonier and Bouguereau—there are no discernible brushstrokes. Yet with Monet, you can see how he applies the paint. You can imagine his hand moving the brush. You admit that it seems kind of interesting. For instance, in Monet's *Impression, Sunrise*, which you remember seeing in 1874 at the first Impressionist exhibition, you note that the brushstrokes mirror a kind of reflection of water. The smokestacks in the distance made you think of how your country rebounded after the shameful defeat in the Franco-Prussian War. Perhaps Monet is depicting how France rebuilt its economy by showing the sunrise over France. It is, you think, rather clever.

Since you have tried your hand at art yourself, you have in the past visited the shop of Père Tanguy (and so has nearly every other artist in Paris). Tanguy is known to be a helpful man, and he is very encouraging to artists, especially those just starting out. You have heard that he often trades supplies for paintings. While you browse in his shop, you notice an odd portrait of Tanguy hanging on the wall. There is a certain likeness, but the image is very flat. Tanguy is painted in very bright colors and looks almost like a paper cutout. He is shown surrounded by a representation of Japanese prints. This seems appropriate, since Tanguy collects Japanese prints, but the effect is strange and off-putting—especially for a *portrait*, you think. You ask the proprietor about this painting and are told that Vincent Van Gogh painted it in 1887. You look at the painting again, noting that you can see the brushstrokes even more clearly than in the Monet paintings at the Durand-Ruel Gallery. They seem frenetic in their application, and the colors seem to have come right out of the tube! This painting by Van Gogh is so different from the art you saw at the Musée de Luxembourg and even Durand-Ruel's Gallery. You have a hard time imagining how this sort of avant-garde nonsense will stand the test of time.

Craving some solidity after your visit to Tanguy's shop, you decide to visit the Panthéon. Here you see the murals that Puvis de Chavannes painted in 1877:

The Childhood of St. Geneviève. You remember how back in 1887 at the Durand-Ruel Gallery you saw other paintings by Puvis de Chavannes—you were so moved by the one titled *The Poor Fisherman* from 1881 that you don't think you will ever forget it. It was powerful in its presentation, but you still wonder what it was about. Bouguereau paints art that is about mythology and classical stories. But what is this poor fisherman doing, and how is he uplifting? And yet you note that in this mural in the Panthéon, the same artist who painted the poor fisherman is celebrating the life of the patron saint of Paris. Should art not lift up (inspire?) those who view it?

As you head home, you are glad you took the time to see these works on a single day. But as you reflect on your day, you realize that everything was so different. There was such a diversity of styles of art that it was dizzying. To steady yourself, you decide to stop at the Café de la Nouvelle-Athènes in order to ponder all that you have seen.

You sit back, take a sip of steaming coffee, and watch the lights chase away the oncoming gloom. You overhear some artists talking. One of them—you think you catch that his name is Seurat—is discussing the scientific properties of color. He keeps mentioning his painting *A Sunday Afternoon on the Island of La Grande Jatte* (1884–86). He is really going on and on about it. You recall that it was displayed in the last Impressionist exhibition of 1886, which you attended. While you listen to the artist expound about color theory, you become mesmerized by his very specific explanations. He advocates that a color can be fully seen only when it is placed next to another color. Each color placement affects the color that is next to it, and so on. Complementary colors placed next to each other will be more vibrant, but similar colors—those next to each other on the color wheel—will seem more muted. You, too, have heard about the color wheel and the properties of complementary colors. That makes you think back to your visit to Tanguy's shop. Was Van Gogh, who used such bright colors, trying to work out a version of scientific color theory as well?

After a few minutes, you pay your bill and, with

hat back atop your head, start for home. It has been a very busy day, and you want to rest up before tomorrow, when you will view the annual Salon of 1888. You are told that there will be a discussion of the prizes that were awarded, and you are excited to attend. It is art and it is Paris, and you are thrilled to be a part of it!

WHAT IS A HISTORICAL ROLE-PLAYING GAME?

Immersive historical role-playing games are an innovative classroom pedagogy that teaches history and related subjects by placing students in moments of heightened historical tension. The class becomes a public body, or private gathering; students, in role, become particular persons from the period and/or members of factional alliances. Their purpose is to advance an agenda and achieve victory objectives through formal speeches, informal debate, negotiations, vote-taking, and conspiracy. After a few preparatory sessions, the game begins, and the students are in charge. The instructor serves as an adviser/arbiter. Outcomes sometimes vary from the history; a debriefing session sets the record straight.

The following is an outline of what you will encounter in this game and what you will be expected to do.

Game Setup

The instructor will explicate the historical context of the game before the game formally begins. During the setup period, you will read several different kinds of material:

- The game book (from which you are reading now), which includes historical background, rules and features of the game, core texts, and essential documents
- A role sheet, describing the historical person you will model in the game and, where applicable, the faction to which you belong
- Supplementary documents or books that, if assigned, will provide additional informa-tion and arguments for use during the game

Read all of this material before the game begins (or as much as possible, catching up once the game is under way). And, just as important, go back and reread these materials throughout the game. A second and third reading while *in role* will deepen your understanding and alter your perspective, for ideas take on a different meaning when seen through the eyes of a particular character. Students who have carefully read the materials and who know well the rules of the game will do better than those who rely on general impressions.

Game Play

Once the game begins, usually one student, randomly chosen, elected, or identified by role, will preside over the class sessions. Your instructor then becomes the Gamemaster (GM) and takes a seat in the back of the room. While not directing the play of the game, the Gamemaster may do any of the following:

- Pass notes to individuals or factions
- Announce important events, some of which may be the result of student actions, others instigated by the GM
- Perform scheduled interventions, sometimes determined by die rolls
- Interrupt proceedings that have gone off track
- Arbitrate play-related controversies

Generally speaking, you are either in a faction or outside the factions as an Indeterminate. Some factions include roles that are significantly differ-ent from one another, while others do not, but all Indeterminates are different from one another: they operate outside the established factions. In games where the factions are tightly-knit groups with fixed objectives, Indeterminates provide the most obvious source of extra support. Cultivating them is, therefore, in the interest of faction mem-bers because one faction will not have the voting strength to prevail without allies. Collaboration and coalition building are at the heart of every game.

The classroom may sometimes be noisy with multiple points of focus because of side conversations, note passing, and players out of their seats. But these practices are also disruptive and can spoil the effect of formal speeches. Nothing is accomplished by trying to talk over the din to persons not listening, so insist upon order and quiet before proceeding.

Always assume, when spoken to by a fellow student on game-related matters—whether in class or out of class—that the person may be speaking to you in role. If you need to address a classmate out of role, employ a visual sign, like crossed fingers, to indicate your changed status. It is inappropriate to trade on out-of-class relationships when asking for support or favors.

Work to balance your emotional investment in your role with the need to treat your classmates with respect. Some specific roles may require you to advocate beliefs with which you personally disagree. While such assignments may seem difficult at first, careful study of your role sheet and the readings should help you develop a greater understanding of why this person thought and acted as he or she did. In a few cases, you may even need to promote ideas that are viewed as controversial or offensive in today's society. Again, always go back to the sources: analyze why those ideas made sense for that particular person in that particular time and place, and then advocate those beliefs as persuasively and effectively as you can. If you ever feel uncomfortable or uncertain about your role, you should feel free to speak with your instructor. Remember also that you will have an opportunity during the debriefing session to discuss the differences between your game character and your personal beliefs or values.

Game Requirements

The instructor will lay out the specific requirements for the class. In general, though, this game will have students perform three distinct activities:

- **Reading and Writing.** This standard academic work is carried on more purposefully because what you read is put to immediate use, and what you write is meant to persuade others to act in preferred ways. The reading load may vary with roles (that done as research is in addition to that done as preparation); the writing requirement is typically a set number of pages per game. In both cases the instructor is free to make adjustments. Papers are often policy statements, but also autobiographies, poems, newspaper articles, clandestine messages, or after-game reflections. Papers often provide the bases of speeches.

- **Public Speaking and Debate.** In most games, every player is expected to deliver at least one formal speech (the length of the game and the size of the class will affect the number of speeches). Debate occurs after a speech is delivered. Debate is impromptu, raucous, and fast-paced, and often results in decisions determined by voting.

- **Strategizing.** Communication with other players is essential. You may find yourselves writing emails, texting, attending out-of-class meetings, or gathering for meals on a fairly regular basis. The purpose of these communications is to lay out a strategy for advancing your agenda and thwarting the agenda of your opponents, or to hatch plots to ensnare individuals who oppose your cause.

Skill Development

This game provides the opportunity to develop a host of academic and life skills:

- Effective writing
- Public speaking
- Problem solving
- Leadership
- Teamwork
- Adaptation to fast-changing circumstances
- Working under pressure with deadlines to meet

2

Historical Background

TIMELINE

1648: The Académie royale de peinture et de sculpture (Royal Academy of Painting and Sculpture) is established under King Louis XIV.

1793: After the French Revolution, "royale" is dropped from the name.

1816: The Academy merges with two other arts organizations to form the Académie des Beaux-Arts; it is still known as the Academy.

1863: Salon des Refusés. Emperor Napoleon III orders a special exhibition of all the "rejected" art.

1874: First Impressionist exhibition.

1888: Academy concludes its annual Salon; the game begins.

HISTORICAL NARRATIVE

The French Academy

Charged with developing and organizing the aesthetic considerations of the art of France, the Académie royale de peinture et de sculpture was established by Louis XIV in 1648. The fourteen lifetime members of the Academy, as it is usually called, set the standards for all art in France. The Academy controlled the training of artists through its school, the École des Beaux-Arts, and showcased the art of its students through an annual Salon—a huge public showing of painting and sculpture. All artists at the school were required to submit work to the annual Salon, which was judged by a jury made up of Academy members who were also recipients of medals at former Salons. The Salon was a major event in the Parisian calendar, and many people attended.

Hierarchies of Art

The Academy developed a hierarchical system of paintings. Since the Academy controlled the École des Beaux-Arts and decided what sort of work could be shown in the annual Salon, this hierarchy dominated the French art scene. History paintings were at the top of the hierarchy because they required artists to demonstrate imagination, education, and technical proficiency. In addition to representing historical French subjects, they could render myths—preferably Greek and Roman—and Christian subjects.

In the Academy's hierarchy, history paintings were followed, in descending order, by portraits, genre scenes (which captured moments of everyday life, usually in rural France), landscapes, and still lifes. This hierarchy indicates that mere observation—inherent in landscape paintings and still lifes—was less valued than conception—a primary feature of history paintings in that they require *education*, as the themes are taken from ancient history and the Bible, and *imagination*, as the artist must conceive of an entire work without copying it from his or her visual field.

Portraiture ranked second in the hierarchy because it involves more than just rendering a likeness; a successful portrait expresses something of the interior character of the subject, which must be brought out carefully by the painter. Portraiture was very popular at the time; some artists supported themselves by painting portraits on commission. Artists also continued to paint landscapes and genre paintings because they were popular with art collectors. This created a market that many artists sought to fill.

The Academy also had certain expectations of how paintings—history paintings in particular—should be composed. For instance, painters were expected to create a clearly delineated foreground, middle ground, and background in a history painting. This allowed for a sense of depth and naturalism in the work. A good example of an artist who follows these rules is Nicolas Poussin, who painted in the seventeenth century. Poussin's *The Burial of Phocion* (1648) is an excellent example of this technique and also a textbook example of the Academy's ideas at this particular time. Poussin chose a classical story. Phocion was a fourth-century B.C.E. statesman in Athens, Greece, wrongly accused of a crime. He was put to death and given a poor-man's burial. Poussin focuses the viewer's attention on the body of Phocion by placing it in the center of the foreground, with light hitting the burial shroud that covers the body as it is carried to the grave. This deliberate foreground is paired with a distinct middle ground, where you can see people doing various activities, and background, where classically inspired buildings dominate the landscape. No one can paint something like *The Burial of Phocion* from life. As a still life, a bowl of lemons can essentially be copied from life. But a history painter must conceive of a scene, research it, and render it with minute detail.

Rococo

To understand the art of 1888 and 1889 Paris, we must first examine its development in the eighteenth century, as well as the changes in the nineteenth century that led up to where our game begins (1888). Rococo was an artistic style favored by the aristocracy, which tended to focus on the pursuit of pleasure. This style was a departure from some of the desires that the Academy was demanding in the seventeenth century. Rococo artists chose to make art more lighthearted in subject.

A typical painting that demonstrates this is Jean-Honoré Fragonard's 1767 painting *The Swing*. In this painting, a girl in a pink dress is being pushed on a swing by a chaperone. A young man, who might be the young woman's beau, is in the lower left-hand corner. The angle of the view of the young man is directed upward to the girl's "dress." She kicks off her shoe in a moment of enjoyment. Several statues of cupid that decorate the garden have their fingers to their lips, imploring us—the viewers—not to spoil the couple's fun and let the chaperone know that he's actually helping the two share an illicit moment. There is no moral message here; the painter is demonstrating a scene of love and playfulness. For more works in the Rococo style, see Watteau, *Pilgrimage to Cythera* (1717) and Boucher, *Louise O'Murphy* (1752).

Neoclassicism

By the middle of the eighteenth-century, a new style developed that coincided with the emergence of the Enlightenment: Neoclassicism. Interest in classical philosophical texts mirrored artists' growing concern with Greek and Roman sculpture. In the art world, Neoclassicism was a reaction against what was now seen as the excesses of the Rococo style. Neoclassicism is a total rejection of this playfulness. The Academy and the artists who painted were, of course, influenced by the politics around them, and many artists turned to themes of civic virtue, the history of ancient Greece and Rome, and the writings of art historians such as Johann Winckelmann, who wrote the first history of ancient Greek art.

They were also inspired by the late eighteenth-century archaeological discoveries of the long-lost cities of Pompeii and Herculaneum. Covered in ash by the explosion of Mount Vesuvius in A.D. 70, the wall paintings, sculptures, and other decorative objects had been almost perfectly preserved. Eighteenth-century excavations of these two sites brought about an understanding of Roman clothing, furniture, and other belongings and fueled the imagination of western Europeans, leading to an intense fervor over this "new" classical style.

The work of Jacques-Louis David epitomizes the Neoclassical style of art, which was a reimagining of the classical art of the Greek and Romans. A student at the École des Beaux-Arts studying under Joseph-Marie Vien, David won the Prix de Rome in 1774 for his painting *Antiochus and Stratonice*. The Prix de Rome was a highly sought-after prize; recipients received an all-expenses-paid five-year stay in Rome to study the art of the ancient Greeks and Romans as well as Renaissance and Baroque masters.

David studied and painted in Rome from 1775 to 1780. He returned to Rome in 1784 to seek inspiration for a royal commission. The result was David's best-known painting, *The Oath of the Horatii*, which was exhibited at the 1785 Salon. The painting is based on a Roman story recorded by Livy. The story is set around 669 B.C.E., when Rome was fighting with the city of Alba. It was decided that the dispute would be settled by having three Roman brothers, the Horatii, fight three brothers from Alba, the Curiatii. Intermarriage between the two families raised the stakes. Despite their possible personal losses, the Horatii pledged to fight for Rome and their family's honor. David showed his imagination by painting a scene that is not described in the traditional story of the Horatii: the moment of the oath they took to their father.

When composing the scene, David chose the triangle, the strongest of all compositional shapes for painting. The men stand firmly in this triangular shape; their muscles ripple down their legs and up their arms. The strength of the men about to fight is symbolized and reflected in this triangular composition, which adds to the idea of the strength of the Horatii brothers. Similarly, the women who are distraught over potentially losing a brother or husband are painted in the form of a triangle, though a softer one. The inclusion of three Roman arches in the background enhances the geometric precision: three arches, three brothers, and the triangular composition.

The background is no longer as deep as in Poussin's *The Burial of Phocion*; the background and foreground are conflated. This tendency to reduce spatial depth is a way to highlight the action and to make it more dramatic. There are no visible brushstrokes in this work, contrary to the works of the Rococo period. David and other Neoclassical painters felt that the "hand of the artist" as seen in visible paint application would distract the viewer from the meaning of the painting.

While not overtly political at its creation, this work came to symbolize French revolutionary ideas when the winds of political change swept through Paris a few years after its debut at the annual Salon of 1785. Later revolutionaries viewed this painting and read the message of personal sacrifice as a rallying cry for their move toward a

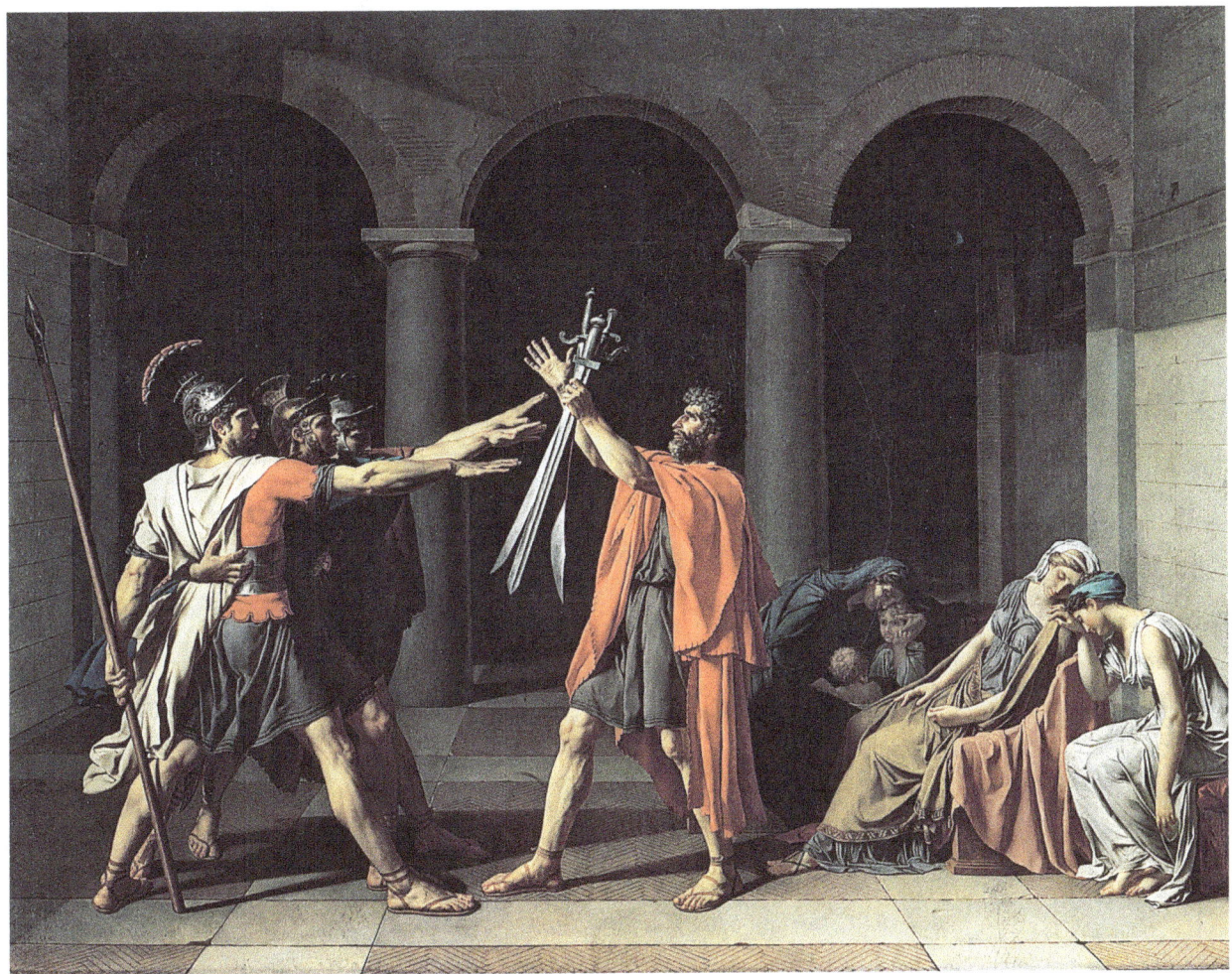

Jacques-Louis David, *The Oath of the Horatii*, 1784, Louvre.

republic. While the style of Neoclassicism dominated the Academy in the years leading up to the Revolution and immediately afterward, the cool rationality of paintings like *The Oath of the Horatii* began to be challenged by other artists, giving way to the period of Romanticism. For more examples of David's Neoclassicism, see David, *Death of Socrates* (1787) and David, *Death of Marat* (1793).

Romanticism

Romanticism sprang from disillusionment about the possibilities and promises of the Enlightenment. The logic and reason that was promised by Enlightenment thinkers and philosophers seemed to be at odds with the political upheaval that was experienced in France during and after the French Revolution. Similarly, the rationality and lack of emotion in the Neoclassical style seemed out of touch with the chaos that ensued in postrevolutionary France. These experiences led in part to a change in art styles at the beginning of the nineteenth century

Romanticism included subjects that described the sublime: the uncontrollable power of nature. Unlike during the Enlightenment period, when the emphasis was placed on reason and the

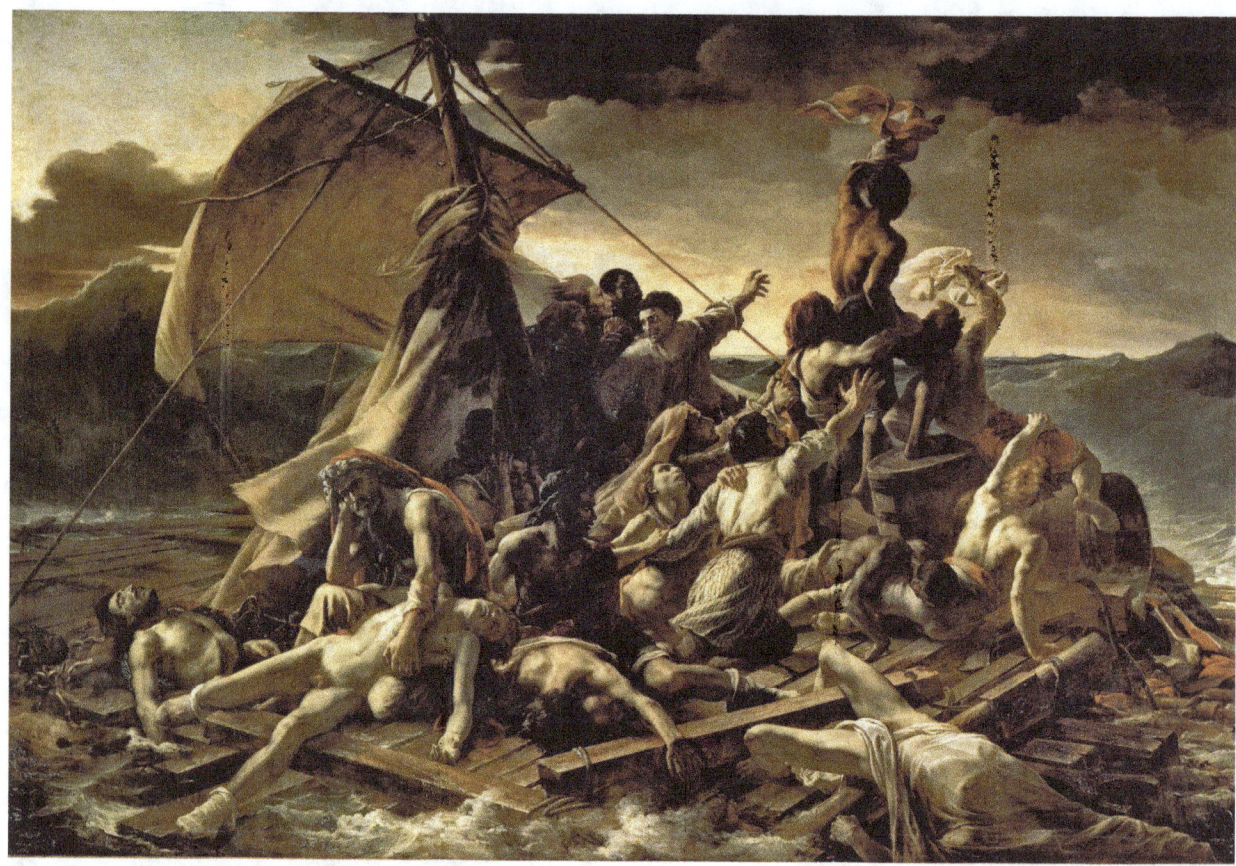

Théodore Géricault, *The Raft of the Medusa*, 1818–19, Louvre.

rational control of the world, the Romantics were drawn to subjects depicting the uncontrollable. Thus, storms in landscapes became popular subjects, showing the power of nature over our ability to control it.

This period of art was also a time in which unspeakable horrors were depicted. In some cases, artists portrayed extreme situations in which most people would never find themselves. Such is the case with one of the most important paintings of the Romantic period in France, Théodore Géricault's *The Raft of the Medusa*, painted between 1818 and 1819 and shown in the 1819 Salon. Measuring more than sixteen by twenty-three feet, Géricault's painting demonstrates the shift in history painting that took place during the Romantic period. This work has been referred to as a "Romantic

manifesto," for it had everything artists were looking for when they began seeking an antithesis to Neoclassical painting.

The Raft of the Medusa refers to the naval frigate *Medusa*, which ran aground off the coast of Africa in 1816. After this grounding, 147 people were stranded and left to fend for themselves on a makeshift raft, on which they drifted at sea for thirteen days before eventually being rescued. Only fifteen people survived the ordeal, and five of these died soon after.

Géricault portrays for the viewer the survivors' plight on the raft. Wanting to get the true horror across, Géricault interviewed the survivors and put into a visual world their tales of brutality, starvation, dehydration, and cannibalism. The entire episode became a scandal for the French government, and the scale of this painting, which is larger than life, created a kind of visual spectacle, in which the viewing of the painting became an event in and of itself.

Part of this visual spectacle of horror was achieved through the composition. If you look closely at the painting, you will notice that bodies—some of them dead—are literally hanging off the raft in the foreground of the painting. Recall the description of the importance of a distinctly delineated foreground, middle ground, and background in Poussin's *The Burial of Phocion*. In *The Raft of the Medusa*, there is none of this clearly delineated space. The limply hanging bodies tilt diagonally into the viewer's space, providing a visual entrance into the painting. There are two large diagonals that intersect and stretch across this very large canvas. The viewer is pulled up along one diagonal to the man who is reaching with a towel or rag with all the force of his body to attempt to get the attention of a very small ship that is depicted on the horizon. In addition to the viewer, everyone on the raft is surging toward that towel in the air. Another diagonal comes from the lower right corner of the painting, up to the mast and the sail that is billowing, attempting to keep the rickety raft afloat.

The Raft of the Medusa retains some of the elements the Academy favored. For instance, the subject is, to an extent, a history painting. However, Géricault moved away from the traditions of the Academy by choosing a subject not steeped in the French past but based on a contemporary event. Also, rather than being about doing one's duty, as in *The Oath of the Horatii*, the painting is primarily emotional. The viewer cannot help but imagine what it would be like to be among those on the raft, hoping to survive. The emotional drama of this painting creates a sensation in a way that is less cerebral and moral than David's Neoclassical canvases. Géricault was searching for a way to tap into the public's emotions. Through its very size and its dramatic presentation, *The Raft of the Medusa* breaks away from the calm and ordered

sense of Neoclassicism. For more on French Romanticism, see Delacroix, *Death of Sardanapalus* (1827), Delacroix, *Massacre at Chios* (1824), and Ingres, *Grand Odalisque* (1814).

Realism

Another aesthetic shift occurred around 1850, when artists began to tire of painting subjects that were so alien to the experience of the art-viewing public. The exotic places, events, and people of the Romantic era came to an end with the advent of Realism. Unlike Romanticism, artists who followed the ideas of Realism desired to paint what one could actually see. Who would really find themselves on a raft, fighting for their life? Who would actually go into a harem to see an odalisque? A statement by the artist Gustave Courbet, whose work follows the tenets of Realism, sums up Realist thought: "I have never seen an angel. Show me an angel, and I'll paint one." (Quoted by Vincent van Gogh in a letter to his brother Theo [July 1885] in *The Letters of Vincent van Gogh*, edited by Ronald de Leeuw [New York: Penguin, 1996], 302.)

Realism is about representing the world that we can actually see. A good example is Courbet's *A Burial at Ornans*, painted in 1850. Measuring over ten feet by twenty-one feet, this is another large-scale painting meant for display in the Salon. Because of the sheer size and the proportions of the figures, viewers almost become part of the funeral procession. The large size suggests that this must be a history painting about the death of a famous person. After all, that would typically be the type of painting that would be seen at the annual Salons. However, as becomes clear after examining the details of the painting, this is not the case. The title of this work is very important for understanding its meaning, for the viewer is witnessing "a" burial—not "the" burial, with a famous name attached. Unlike *The Burial of Phocion*, which was a depiction of the interment of an important ancient Athenian statesman, we have no clue in the title of the work to indicate whose burial we are seeing. However, there are clues in the painting that suggest that this is, in fact, an important burial. For instance, there are many priests and clergy lined up on the left side of the painting. A man is very prominently displayed near the hole of the grave wearing the very distinctive costume of blue stockings. This is an important element in the painting, for these types of blue stockings were an eighteenth-century piece of clothing worn by men for special occasions.

But who has died?

To answer this question, you must look at the grave in the center foreground of the painting. It is here that the viewer "enters" the painting. The subject of the painting is *not* the burial of a famous person; the grave is *our grave*. The viewer is for whom the grave awaits. Through the sheer number of church representatives, the reference to a costume reserved for special occasions, and the placement of the grave at the base of the viewer's space, Courbet is suggesting that the death of every person—even the common man—should be commemorated as an important event. Although some scholars have suggested that it was painted as a commemoration of Courbet's uncle's death, it could very easily represent the burial of anyone in the village of Ornans, which is in the Franche-Comté, near the Swiss border.

In response to Courbet's decision to make a depiction of an everyday funeral the size of a typical Salon history painting, many people were outraged and felt that Courbet was attempting to destroy traditional painting. However, it was not just the subject matter that led people to decry this painting; the enormous canvas actually appears quite flat. Courbet employs several methods of both suggesting and then denying a sense of space in the work. For instance, the crucifix at the left of the painting appears to be off in the distance, situated in the partition of the cliffs that make up the background. However, if you look closely at the pole on which the crucifix is attached, your eye follows down to realize that one of the clergy is holding it. This clergyman is in the foreground of the painting and thus your eye is pulled back to the front, denied a sense of depth. Thus, the crucifix that seems at first to be in the background is actually in the foreground of the painting.

Courbet also lines all his figures up, left to right, in the same overall arrangements as the cliffs in the background, in a shape that is described as a bit of an S curve. This same curvature is seen in the spine of the dog that is placed in the lower right of the painting. This "flattening" of the canvas—the denial of spatial depth in the painting—offended the Academy and traditional artists as much as the subject matter. Just as the painting is about the burial of a common citizen of Ornans, Courbet believed it was the "burial of Romanticism." Courbet is an example of an avant-garde artist working in the middle of the century. He is advancing art by pushing the limits of what is acceptable.

In 1855, Courbet submitted fourteen paintings for exhibition at the Exposition Universelle, an international exhibition that was to be held on the Champs-Élysées in Paris. The exposition was an attempt to outdo London's 1851 Great Exhibition at the Crystal Palace, a large exposition hall that was built nearly entirely of glass. Three of Courbet's works were rejected for exhibition, presumably for a "lack of space." However, these were his major canvases, including *A Burial at Ornans* and another important large-scale work, *The Artist's Studio*.

Courbet decided he would not be denied the chance to show his work during this special exposition. So he created his own exhibition space called the Pavilion of Realism, which he was able to erect right next to the government-backed exposition exhibition. To advertise this "alternative" to the Exposition Universelle, Courbet published a manifesto titled "On Realism," put posters all over France advertising his art, and charged one franc for admission. It has been suggested that Courbet made nearly 4,000 francs through this enterprise. Its importance for the art world, however, was the idea that one could display works in a space that was an alternative to the state-sponsored, traditional Salon—and people would still go to see it. Up until this point, no one had dared exhibit anywhere other than in the official Salon. Other examples of French Realism include Courbet, *The Stonebreakers* (1850), Courbet, *The Artist's Studio* (1855), and Millet, *The Gleaners* (1857).

The Salon des Refusés

Every year, there were more works of art submitted to the annual Salon than could be accepted. But in 1863, there was a larger percentage of *rejected* works than ever before. Having your work rejected from the Salon was difficult for artists. Being refused admittance to the Salon meant less exposure to the Parisian public, which would severely diminish the possibility of selling to collectors or receiving commissions. With such a large number of rejected works, the public began to wonder what could be so wrong with the paintings. They grew curious and started to demand to see them.

Hearing this growing clamor to see the rejected works, Napoleon III's government decided to allow the works to be shown in what it thought would be a sort of anti-Salon. It became known as the Salon des Refusés (Salon of the Refused). All the works that were rejected were displayed in this dubious Salon in 1863. Upon viewing the works in this exhibition, most of the public agreed that the rejected art did not belong in the official annual Salon. However, others—including a number of young artists—did not agree. Some of these artists later became part of the Impressionist group.

Édouard Manet's painting *Déjeuner sur L'Herbe* (*Luncheon on the Grass*) stands out among the works at the Salon des Refusés. Many people today consider it one of the most important paintings of the nineteenth century, if not of all time. It depicts a nude woman, picnicking outdoors with two men, who are dressed in contemporary Parisian outfits. Some have interpreted the location of the picnic as the Bois de Boulogne, which was a large park on the outskirts of Paris, commonly known as a place where one could easily solicit a prostitute or engage in illicit sexual

activity after dark. Manet shines a light on this behavior in a most startling way.

Manet's composition is based on a famous painting by Raphael called *The Judgment of Paris* (now lost, it survives only in engravings). Raphael's painting depicts the judgment of the most beautiful of the Greek gods by Paris, the Trojan prince. To the lower right of Raphael's painting was a group of three water nymphs in the same position as our three main characters in Manet's painting. By including this compositional triumvirate, Manet references Raphael's *Judgment of Paris*, which is about beauty. However, Manet modernizes its treatment.

The nude woman, Victorine Meurent, was known to the Parisian art community, as she was a model for many artists. She was also the model in another famous painting by Manet, *Olympia*, also from 1863. In both paintings, she stares out at the viewer; she confronts one directly, not shielding her eyes. But it is not just the position of her face that confronts the viewer. Manet is very confrontational in the *way* that he paints. In *Luncheon*, there is a flattening of the model's body; there is a lack of shadow and modeling in her flesh. She appears to be almost all one color and outlined against the dark background. Her depiction is like the painting as a whole. It is difficult to understand the spatial relationships in the painting because the woman in the background is really too large for her placement. What's more, space is unnaturally condensed. In the same way that Courbet played with the notion of spatial depth in *A Burial of Ornans*, Manet manipulates the sense of depth in *Luncheon on the Grass*. People also commented on the "sloppy" still life in the lower left of the painting, where you can see the paint strokes of the picnic lunch.

Most critics decried this painting for its vulgarity in subject, which was an overt reference to prostitution, and the way in which it was painted, with heavy brushstrokes and a lack of modeling and color on the human body. But for the artists who would go on to form the Impressionists, this painting was a wonder. Artists like Claude Monet and Edgar Degas found in Manet a fresh, honest, and *modern* depiction of subjects, which to them was the beginning of something new and exciting.

The Rise of Impressionism

Courbet's Pavilion of Realism in 1855 and the Salon des Refusés in 1863 demonstrated that alternative venues for displaying art were possible in Paris. In addition, the political situation in France beginning in 1870 had a profound impact on artists. In 1870, France invaded Prussia, but was unsuccessful in the attempt. In September 1870, the Prussians laid siege to Paris, which fell in January 1871. The treaty ending the Franco-Prussian War required the payment of a huge indemnity and the loss of the border provinces of Alsace and Lorraine to Prussia. After further tumult, including the short rule of Paris by the radical left-wing Commune, the Third Republic was established.

The government of the Third Republic was generally conservative, especially in regard to the arts. It attempted to bolster the reputation of the Academy. One step in this reassertion of authority was the limiting of the number of works shown in the annual Salon. This restriction led a group of artists to organize themselves as the Société Anonyme des artistes, peintres, sculpteurs, graveurs, etc. In April 1874, approximately two weeks before the opening of the Academy's Salon, the group opened an exhibition of their art on the second floor of 35, Boulevard des Capucines, the former studio of the famed photographer Nadar.

Thirty artists contributed around two hundred works. In art historical scholarship, the emphasis tends to be on the avant-garde nature of the works exhibited, but the show also included artists with more traditional styles. Apparently Edgar Degas argued for their inclusion, whereas Claude Monet and Camille Pissarro thought otherwise. However, this move paid off, as the inclusion of traditional art gave the exhibition some academic weight. On the other hand, the comparison of the more conservative pieces with the avant-garde works—such as

those by Monet, Degas, Cézanne, Morisot, Renoir, and Pissarro—showcased these new efforts all the more clearly. This was the first of eight such shows organized between 1874 and 1886.

This show came to be known as the first Impressionist exhibition. It took this name from Monet's painting *Impression, Sunrise* (1872), which encapsulates the Impressionist interest in the atmospheric conditions that affect light and color in a landscape. This was also the first time that artists painted outdoors in order to catch the momentary aspects of light shifts on their surroundings. The Industrial Revolution, which brought about the expansion of train lines and tubes of premixed paint, allowed artists to travel to areas outside Paris to paint outdoors, or *en plein air*.

It has been argued that Monet chose to depict the busy port of Le Havre in order to show France on the comeback from the Franco-Prussian War. We see a harbor with many ships moving in and out, which demonstrates that trade and thus the French economy are on a positive trajectory after the war. It is also a sunrise, which connotes hope to those in France. Capturing the effects of light on the water in the hazy mist of morning makes this a good example of Impressionism. It is also a modern painting, for it is a contemporary view of the harbor in 1872—the year in which it was painted. Thus, it is not a history painting; rather, it is a painting about painting, and follows the mantra that developed among Impressionist artists: "Art for art's sake!" This means that art can be about art—about the act of painting. Art does not have to have a moral message, make viewers live a better life, or teach viewers about a particular event in French history. Instead, viewers can see this harbor in France and remark on the colors and light represented.

But what did the public think about this alternative art exhibit? Most Parisians—spurred on by conservative government critics—found the art in the first Impressionist exhibition laughable. Furthermore, many art critics responded with scathing reviews. Louis Leroy compared Monet's painting to unfinished wallpaper. Leroy went on to say that the artist could not even paint a true sunrise but could only offer an "impression" of one.

Some critics were more positive about the exhibit, which serves to demonstrate the diversity of styles and attitudes that were developing in Paris in the years immediately prior to 1888. Several critics noted that France needed new direction in painting and that there was little that was new in the previous year's Salon. There were hopes that the artists who exhibited in this new show could propel French art in new directions and possibly help pull the country out of the depths of despair after its loss in the Franco-Prussian War. While much has been made of the negative reviews, the exhibition actually received much praise.

The first Impressionist exhibition proved to be a seismic shift in the art world of Paris, as these artists proved that the annual Salon's approval was not necessary to make a name for oneself as an artist. In addition, many works were sold at the exhibition, which helped move art into the realm of commodity. Perhaps sales were more important than prestige and critical renown.

Neo-Impressionism and Postimpressionism

Impressionism opened the way for artists to render works in a plethora of avant-garde styles that presented ever-greater challenges to the Salon as a bastion of traditional aesthetics. Around 1886, the term "Neo-Impressionism" was coined by the art critic Félix Fénéon in reference to the style of painting developed by Georges Seurat, who was influenced by Charles Henry and others who wrote on color theory. Soon artists like Paul Signac and Camille Pissarro adopted this style.

Seurat used the color wheel and individual daubs of paint to create his *Sunday Afternoon on the Island of La Grande Jatte*, which took him two years to paint, from 1884 to 1886. To make colors seem more vibrant, he placed daubs of complementary colors next to each other. To make colors blend, he placed daubs of adjacent colors, making the transition less jarring.

Van Gogh used color even more adventurously

and much more crudely. As noted in the prologue, the portrait of *Père Tanguy* that Van Gogh completed in 1887 has bright, fully saturated colors, as if taken directly from the tube of paint. The brushstrokes are clearly visible.

Paul Gauguin continued the tradition of flattening out the canvas that we saw most recently in Manet's painting *Luncheon on the Grass*. In Gauguin's 1888 *Still Life with Three Puppies*, the puppies are in the upper part of the painting, drinking milk from a pan. Three glasses are placed below the pan, presumably on a table, and some pears are arranged at the bottom of the canvas. The entire floor or table is pushed to the foreground. There is no sense of middle ground or background. Further flattening out the canvas is a black outline of each puppy and object. This also helps to flatten each object. A repeating pattern on the table also flattens the canvas, as any repeating pattern on a flat surface accentuates the two-dimensionality of that surface, like wallpaper does.

The Current Situation

Currently a fairly stable, moderate republican government is in place, seeking to bolster its position through the arts. This government seeks to foster republicanism through major public commissions, including the purchase of work shown in the annual Salon for display in provincial museums and the Musée du Luxembourg in Paris.

In 1881, the government stepped away from direct administration of the annual Salon and gave that responsibility to the Société des Artistes Français, which was composed of artists who previously received Salon awards of third-class medals or higher. This means that the Salon is still controlled by artists who are faithful to the Academy and academic painting, and who strive to uphold traditional painting.

While the Salon continues to dominate the art scene, a few private galleries are available for group shows, and a handful of dealers—including Paul Durand-Ruel—have begun sponsoring individual or group exhibitions. There are other art dealers in

Paris as well, including Georges Petit, who seek to display works that will sell, having seen the success of the Impressionist exhibitions.

The 1888 Salon

The jury for the 1888 Salon accepted 2,586 paintings. Adding the sculpture entries, the total number of works rose to 4,764. The number of works each artist could show was limited to one or two, which meant that there were a great many artists showing, and they had limited space to show their work. Some artists would like to see future Salons allowing fewer artists, so that those accepted could show more work.

One of the major medal winners at the 1888 Salon was Édouard Detaille's *The Dream*. Detaille's painting depicts a bivouac of French soldiers on a training maneuver. Above them floats a vision of the military glories of the past, including the soldiers of the French Revolution, Napoléon, and the Restoration of the monarchy. Given the pending reinstatement of conscription, the politics behind this painting are obviously highly nationalistic and supportive of the political right.

While traditional artists felt that this was a wise choice for a medal of honor at the Salon, many avant-garde artists and critics found the bestowal of such a grand award on this painting to be a symbol of all that is wrong in the world of art. This Reacting to the Past game opens after the awards are bestowed on the recipients of the 1888 Salon. Characters in the game meet at the Salon to discuss the awards and the paintings displayed. The works that represent the art that was included in the Salon include Detaille's *The Dream*, which, along with other works from the Salon, can be accessed on a password-protected site provided by your instructor.

3
The Game

Aesthetics is at the center of the game. The main debate is between advocates of traditional art, which espouses realism, naturalism, technique, and use of perspective, and the varied artists of the Avant-Garde, who want change. However, this is not a simple argument. The artists of the Academy remain devoted to standards, some of which were set in the late seventeenth century, but they all experiment within these constraints. The avant-garde wants change, but its individual members differ greatly on what that change should entail. Some espouse unnatural color choices and a sense of flattened space. Others want to create art that draws viewers into a fantasy world. Still others place the science of color theory first and foremost.

Contemporary art historians tend to ignore late nineteenth-century artists who embraced traditionalism. Instead, they focus more on the avant-garde. This has led to a potential misunderstanding of the power structures at that time. It is true that the Academy was beginning to lose its stranglehold on artistic production in France, but it still controlled the most prestigious venues. This allowed it to dictate artistic taste.

Art criticism is also very important in this period. Many critics were tied to specific artists and had preconceived notions of how art should look. Rare was the critic who came to an exhibition unsure of how he felt about the work displayed there (nearly all critics were male). Art was in many ways a national pastime in France. Some players may feel that the critics should be more open-minded, but this simply was not the case in 1888 and 1889. The critics reflect the main themes in art criticism that would have appeared in various publications in Paris at the time. They are all very savvy and have predetermined thoughts and feelings about the artists in the game. At the outset, none of them are unshakably focused on a single artist, but in the course of the game, they must select individual artists on which to bestow their favor, so artists must speak persuasively to win their affections.

The commodification of art is the final central issue. The Impressionists showed that the government did not have complete proprietary interest over the business of art. Before 1881, the government usually sponsored the annual Salon, meaning that it also held sway over the art that was accepted each year. The government acted as the main buyer for artists and bought what was shown in the Salons. If you were not shown in a Salon, then you would not sell. However, the Impressionists, with their eight independent exhibitions between 1874 and 1886, demonstrated that artists could sell art on their own or through gallery owners or dealers. Dealers represented the economic side of the art world that was evolving at the time.

SKILLS AND LEARNING OUTCOMES

Modernism versus Traditionalism: Art in Paris, 1888–1889 emphasizes skills in visual analysis of images, rhetoric, writing, and oral communication. It also stresses critical thinking and analytic reading. Players will read art criticism from the late nineteenth century and will need to apply that criticism to the art that they are discussing. In order to do this, they must develop skills in visual literacy and critical seeing.

Players must expand their ability to talk about art. Once they have received roles, they must begin *explaining* "their" art. Soon, debate will begin, which means that they will need to *justify* their ideas about art. They cannot just explain why they paint what they paint; they need to explain why what they do makes "good art." During the final session, players must stage a series of art exhibitions to accompany the 1889 Exposition Universelle. This will allow them to explain their ideas about art to a larger audience.

As in all reacting games, an emphasis is placed on the development of speaking, writing, and reasoning, and the deep understanding of a specific historic moment. Reacting also highlights several skills that have been identified by the Association of American Colleges and Universities as "Essential Learning Outcomes" for higher education. These include teamwork and problem solving, inquiry and analysis, critical and creative thinking, and written and oral communication.

RULES AND PROCEDURES

The artists in this game are proud and confident. They have nothing to hide about their aesthetic preferences and should voice their opinions about art as long as they understand and can articulate why they like what they like. In this, players must try to divorce themselves from the contemporary, individualistic ethos that celebrates "I like it because I like it" as a valid position. Players must work hard to understand the intellectual basis for their aesthetic preferences.

OBJECTIVES AND VICTORY CONDITIONS

Specific objectives for victory vary by role. By 1888–89, not all Impressionists were interested in the same thing, and likewise, even some Academy members had different ideas on how the annual Salons should be run. However, every artist in the game shares one key victory objective: to sell art. Every artist realizes that this has become an essential index of success. Thus, all artists must think about how to best position themselves to sell art at the 1889 Exposition Universelle.

Critics want the artists that they support to sell as much art as possible. The two dealers want to outdo each other in sales. Academy members want to be sure that they, through their annual Salon, remain the focal point of the art world and need to figure out how to keep most of the attention on themselves, for there will be many other venues displaying art at the exposition that may draw attention away from their annual exhibition.

While additional victory objectives are present for all characters in the game, none of them can be achieved without interacting and talking to one another in the course of the game. *It is impossible to win without engaging with the other characters in the context of the game.* All players must ask questions, listen to speeches, and seek out other characters in order to achieve the outlined victory objectives.

DISCUSSION PROTOCOL

During the first session, **William-Adolphe Bouguereau**, who was the president of the Salon of 1888, should preside. Although the Salon is over, there may be some people who want to discuss the medals that were awarded at the Salon, most specifically the medal of honor that was awarded to Édouard Detaille's *The Dream*. Subsequent days are more flexible, but the podium rule is in effect, so everyone should be able to present prepared speeches. Bouguereau may choose to continue to preside if no one objects. If Bouguereau is indisposed, **Jean-Louis Ernest Meissonier** should preside.

The final game session, which features all the exhibitions that accompany the Exposition Universelle of 1889, may be quite chaotic, since several exhibitions will be running simultaneously. The degree to which players are able to bring some order and clarity to their individual or group presentations on this day will determine their ability to win this part of the game. All players have other objectives, but selling as much art as possible during the final session should remain of paramount importance.

CRITIC TICKETS

Critics may elevate artists through positive reviews. These are represented by Critic Tickets, which should be presented along with speeches during game session 4. Critics should do this publicly and with flourish. The name of the recipient should be placed on the ticket. (Critic Tickets are attached to critics' role sheets.)

Recipients of Critic Tickets are assured **one automatic sale** in 1889.

In addition, the good press surrounding these artists brings additional interest. This means that any show featuring an artist holding a Critic Ticket is ensured **one additional sale.** This is the "Halo Effect."

Note: If a Critic Ticket holder participates in multiple shows, the critic must designate *one* show to be the beneficiary of the Halo Effect.

Note: If a Critic Ticket holder decides to be in a solo show, the extra sale remains with the recipient. Thus, this artist is ensured **two automatic sales.**

ART SHOWS IN 1889

There are *four* possible ways for artists to show their works. For any of these, a maximum of ten artists may show together.

The 1889 Salon

The most renowned venue is the 1889 Salon, which will be organized by the members of the Société des Artistes Français. This definitely includes **Bouguereau, Meissonier, Jean-Léon Gérôme,** and **Jules Breton.** They will be joined by a new member of the Academy, who they will name by session 4.

These artists are determined to stage a magnificent show, but they are struggling to decide how many artists to show and how many paintings each invited artist may display. Finally, they must decide which artists they deem worthy of consideration. They are open to including the works of artists who are considered more traditional.

Nothing rivals the annual Salon in terms of prestige and sales. The members of the Société des Artistes Français plan on taking advantage of the thousands of visitors to the exposition by staging the annual Salon at the Grand Palais on the Champs-Élysées, which is on the other side of the Seine from the exposition grounds. Foreign buyers will flock to it, as will government officials interested in dispensing lucrative and prestigious government commissions. Consequently, the Salon yields **at least two sales** and **one government commission.**

The GM randomly distributes these sales to the artists who show in the Salon. Consequently, the organizers may want to keep the number of participants low in order to maximize the chances that they will make sales. Thus, even artists who do not consider themselves staunch traditionalists should be interested in showing at the Salon. Anyone may submit works to the 1889 Salon, but those works must be accepted by the Salon jury. Artists who want to get their work into the Salon should approach members of the Academy in order to plead their case.

The Salon show will be displayed by projection using the classroom computer and projector system. No one else may use this projection system; it is for the Salon only. This represents their visibility and power.

Gallery Shows

There are two prominent art dealers: **Durand-Ruel** and **Georges Petit**. Both of these dealers have been granted display spaces at the exposition to take advantage of the many visitors that will come to see the events. They are interested in selling lots of art, and they are eager to assume responsibility for organizing the logistics and publicity for shows in their exhibition halls. Shows that are staged by dealers tend to feature like-minded artists who reflect some shared aesthetic.

These shows enjoy a greater likelihood for sales because of the efforts of the gallery owners, so every show organized by a dealer results in **at least two sales**. These two sales are NOT necessarily for the same artist unless a gallery owner stages a one-man retrospective.

Shows mounted by dealers may be displayed on laptop computers.

Group Shows

Dealers can't help everyone. Consequently, like-minded artists with similar aesthetics may band together into group shows. These are simple affairs that are usually staged in cafés. They are not part of the annual Salon, but showing in a group tends to increase foot traffic and sales. In addition, the presence of multiple artists united by a theme may help artists who have difficulty explaining their work.

Artists may decide to flock together in order to offer a group show along the lines of past exhibitions, such as the Salon des Refusés and the first Impressionist exhibition, but they must consider such an affiliation carefully. They should only pair themselves with artists who share their artistic vision. In order to determine who these artists are, they must listen very carefully to the speeches by the different artists to see if they agree with their thoughts.

Artists who decide to stage a group show need to figure out how to display their work. If they like, they may display their work on a single laptop, but they should consider other means as well.

Individual Shows

Some artists just can't seem to catch a break. No one understands the power of their art. This may be depressing, but they are determined to maintain their integrity. They would rather be independent than show with others who want them to compromise their aesthetic or artistic ideals.

Artists who find themselves in such a situation can stage tiny shows in small stalls or in their studios. Because of the limited means and space, the ambitions of these shows are quite limited: these artists are trying to sell enough work to allow them to eat and buy paint (and not necessarily in that order).

This might seem like desperation, but it might not be. During the exposition, Paris will be full of people interested in art. Buyers might wander in to see these works, and if some of them—even *one* of them—purchases a piece, the artist can buy bread and cheese and wine *for months*!

No laptops may be a part of these shows. These artists must figure out ways to attract potential buyers—or maybe just some observers. These shows will be relatively easy to set up compared to the others, but they will be less glitzy.

MAXIMIZING SALES

If gallery shows are remarkably well staged and the dealers, artists, and supportive critics are good at explaining the work on display, they may attract additional buyers. This creates some incentive for exclusivity. If a group show is very large, the benefits brought by the authority of the Salon, Critic Tickets, and hardworking dealers become diluted.

Summary of Art Sale Mechanics

The canvases on display are representative works; buyers are not purchasing individual works of art. Thus, if more work by an individual artist is purchased than is actually hanging in a particular show, that is acceptable.

Money is no object for the buyers, so no one should worry about it. Sales are determined in several ways. If chance is involved, the GM will resolve the sale with a die roll.

Following is a summary of the sources of different sales:

1. Critic Tickets receive one automatic sale for each ticket.
2. Critic Tickets have a Halo Effect, which adds an additional automatic sale to one show.
3. The 1889 Salon receives two automatic sales and one government commission.
4. Gallery shows staged by dealers receive two automatic sales.
5. Well-staged and attended shows will likely attract additional buyers.
6. Shows in which artists are able to explain their work with clarity and accuracy will likely attract additional buyers.

If the Halo Effect benefits a show with multiple artists, an artist other than the Critic Ticket holder may get the Halo Effect sale.

Avoid Anachronism

Artists *may not* show works that were made after 1889. They must carefully research their works and display only those pieces that were completed *before* 1889. Every artist role sheet lists a few of these works, but these are by no means exhaustive lists.

BASIC OUTLINE OF THE GAME

The schedule is broken down into three parts. First, there are several sessions devoted to preparing

players. These sessions focus on developing elementary skills in how to "read" art as well as providing an understanding of the historical context of the game. Then there is the game itself, which culminates in the staging of various exhibitions that accompany the Exposition Universelle of 1889. Finally, there is a session devoted to debriefing.

Preparatory Session 1: Historical Context

Reading to do for class:

All of the gamebook except the core documents. Pay particular attention to the historical narrative.

In-class work:

Review the historical context, with a general discussion of art in the nineteenth century.
Receive role sheets and roster.

Optional Preparatory Session: How to Read Art

Reading to do for class:

The gamebook's Appendix A on formal analysis.

In-class work:

Learn the basic elements of formal analysis, critical analysis, and art history.

Preparatory Session 2: Introductions

Reading to do for class:

The core documents—written and visual—in the gamebook. These include examples of art criticism as well as a few selected images. You should plan to examine each of the four images noted in the visual documents section very closely, reading them using the visual analysis (formal analysis) terms in Appendix A. You should also reread the character list and prepare an introduction of your role to the class.

In-class work:

Examine, discuss, and interpret the paintings listed in the visual documents, applying lessons of formal analysis and historical context.
Introduce yourself in role. After the analysis of the paintings, all characters will

introduce themselves by name and aesthetic style by displaying and discussing one recent work of art. Suggested works to choose appear in the role sheets. Artists can use this opportunity to familiarize themselves with a single piece of work to deepen their understanding of their role and their place in the artistic debates of the era. These presentations—in character but before actual debate—will help players understand the many styles of the time. This should give everyone a chance to see who is in the room and to begin to guess at some basic alignments (who is conservative, who is radical, etc.).

Critics and dealers will also introduce themselves, but not extensively. However, it is important that both critics and dealers show a work of art that matches their past views on art (work they have in the past admired or exhibited). Artists need to understand critics' and dealers' tastes and aesthetic preferences, and then seek them out.

Game Session 1: At the 1888 Salon

The game opens immediately after prizes are given out at the Salon of 1888. **Bouguereau** is in charge of the Salon discussions, as he is the president of the Salon jury. Artists, regardless of their artistic affiliation, come to the annual Salons, and here they have all gathered. There may be some people who want to discuss the medals that were awarded at the Salon, most specifically the medal of honor that was awarded to Édouard Detaille's *The Dream*.

Several of the artists who hold lifetime appointments to the Academy, including **Bouguereau**, **Gérôme**, **Meissonier**, and **Breton**, will want to speak in defense of the awarding of the medal of honor to *The Dream*. These artists should also use this opportunity to present their own work to a broad audience, perhaps comparing it favorably to *The Dream*. Since these masters show their work

hors concours (not part of prize competition), they might even slyly suggest that their work is actually *better* than Detaille's.

In addition to his speech about art, **Bouguereau**, who is presiding over the day's events, will likely have some sad news for those gathered about the death of Gustave Boulanger, holder of seat number 9 on the Academy.

Critics **André Michel** and **Joséphin Péladan** may want to discuss what they find appealing—or not so appealing—in the 1888 Salon. They do not have to give their full Critic Ticket speech, but they should make some comments about the art in the Salon.

The formal speeches by members of the Academy will be followed by prominent artists who do not currently hold Academy seats, including **Pierre Auguste Renoir**, **Pierre Puvis de Chavannes**, and **Gustave Moreau**. **John Singer Sargent** and **James McNeill Whistler** may also speak, or they may want to wait until session 2. These artists have very different artistic visions and styles, yet they are all interested in becoming members of the Academy.

Since Gustave Boulanger has died, his seat is now open, and Academy members must decide who will be added to their ranks, and announce this decision by the *fourth game session* at the latest. Thus, **Renoir**, **Puvis de Chavannes**, and **Moreau** should include in their speech reasons why they deserve a seat on the Academy, which must include discussions of their own works of art. Most of the other artists in the game would not want to be part of the Academy or have a seat on it. If they try to do so, it would be considered a violation of their victory objectives.

All artists should feel free to ask questions. Critics and dealers should be particularly inquisitive, as they need to start identifying artists with interesting work as well as those who are capable of clearly articulating their aesthetic.

After the session breaks up, the members of the Academy should meet (perhaps even out of class) to decide who, among the gathered artists, should take the vacant seat in the Academy. (The prominent artists previously mentioned are the most likely recipients.) This honor should be announced with great fanfare. If you run out of time in session 1, the remaining scheduled speakers may present in session 2.

Game Session 2: The Impressionists and the American Artists Respond

At the outset, dealers **Petit** and **Durand-Ruel** should circulate **one-page broadsides** expressing their opinions about the presentations given during the first session. They should ask a lot of questions of those artists and critics who speak. Critics should ask questions as well. Critics can also submit broadsides or copies of articles that they published in art periodicals. (A broadside is a one-sided promotional poster that includes both images and writing.)

During this session, the artists who continue to adhere most closely to the label "Impressionist"— including **Monet**, **Degas**, **Berthe Morisot**, **Mary Cassatt**, **Whistler**, and **Sargent**—will have an opportunity to speak. These artists are no longer as radical as they once appeared. Indeed, some of the works in the 1888 Salon had Impressionist elements. In fact, both Monet and Morisot had work accepted in past Salons. However, Degas is a tough critic of the Academy and the Salon and would never deign to show in it. The critic **Joris-Karl Huysmans** may wish to speak in support of the Impressionists to help their position. All critics and dealers should ask questions of all artists.

Game Session 3: The Avant-Garde Artists Respond

At the outset, dealers **Petit** and **Durand-Ruel** should circulate a second set of **one-page broadsides** expressing their opinions about the artists who presented their work during the previous session. Dealers and critics should continue asking questions.

This session gives the artists who are on the margins of the Parisian art world an opportunity to speak. These artists on the edge of innovation include **Paul Gauguin**, **Paul Cézanne**, **Vincent van**

Gogh, **Henri de Toulouse-Lautrec**, **Georges Seurat**, **Paul Signac**, and **Camille Pissarro**. Their work is even further removed from the Academy than that of the Impressionists.

The critics **G.-Albert Aurier** and **Félix Fénéon** greatly admire the avant-garde art. They may wish to speak today as well.

At the end of the session, anyone interested in staging a group show in 1889 without the cooperation of dealers or the Salon should make an announcement in an attempt to attract collaborators.

Game Session 4: Planning for the Exposition Universelle of 1889

At the outset of this session, members of the Academy should announce the rules for the Salon of 1889. They should also announce which artist has been chosen to fill the vacant seat in the Academy if they have not done so previously.

Dealers **Petit** and **Durand-Ruel** must give formal speeches, announcing the names of the artists they plan on showing in their galleries in 1889. Dealers must also explain why they chose these artists and show and analyze specific works of art.

All critics should give their formal **Critic Ticket speeches today**. More than one artist can receive a Critic Ticket. Critic Tickets will facilitate planning for the 1889 exposition. Everyone should remember that a Critic Ticket brings with it a Halo Effect. Individual artists may receive multiple Critic Tickets.

Artists who will show as part of groups either at the Salon or in galleries should meet in order to start planning their exhibitions. Critics who support these artists should join them. Other artists (and the critics who support them) may choose to stage group shows with artists who share similar qualities. The names of any artists who decide to stage group shows must be announced at the end of this session. Any remaining artists must stage solo shows.

Staging showings of art can be a complicated

business. Thus, any remaining time (*and extensive time outside regular sessions*) should be devoted to planning the art shows.

Game Session 5: Exposition Universelle of 1889

Groups and individuals stage their exhibitions in conjunction with the Exposition Universelle. The entrance to the exposition grounds is under the Eiffel Tower, which has been built for this very purpose. This will be a major event in Paris, and it will draw many people from all over the world. Who knows who might show up? Artists, critics, and dealers will need to be on hand to explain their work and the work produced by artists they admire. Major sales are possible; be prepared to explain the art you espouse.

In order to maximize sales, artists—and the critics and dealers who support them—should try to build up their credibility and excitement about the contributions their work makes to the future of art in the days leading up to the exposition.

Final Session: Debriefing

Before this session, the GM will tabulate any sales that took place during the exposition. In this postmortem, everyone has an opportunity to reveal their motives and strategies for achieving victory. In addition, the instructor provides information about how the game both adhered to and deviated from historical events. Finally, the instructor provides some information about what happened next.

ASSIGNMENTS

All players must give at least one formal speech, accompanied by an essay, about art. This means that it will be necessary for students to learn how to look closely and think about visual material critically. In our culture, we encounter many images every day, yet we rarely look at them critically. For this game, you will learn about visual analysis, also called formal analysis. This is a tool of art historians, who look at paintings and talk about their composition—how artists use line, color, space, volume, and light to create certain effects—and what that composition means. Use the historical context essay and the formal analysis components in Appendix A when writing your speeches.

Because this is an art game, when you give a speech, you must do so with images. You will need to talk to your instructor about how to project images alongside your speech and how to submit them in your paper, but images are essential. They are considered a primary text in the same way as is art criticism from the period. Written texts and visual images are essential elements to study and use in the game. Some important examples of images to become familiar with are in the Core Texts and Documents section of this gamebook, but you should also spend a significant amount of time examining images that are mentioned in this gamebook in the prologue and historical narrative, as well as any images that are listed in your role sheet.

Artists

Artists promote their personal artistic visions. As noted in the Basic Outline of the Game, artists will speak on certain days. The Academy artists speak first, then the Impressionists and American artists, and then the Avant-Garde artists. To accompany their speeches, artists must display and discuss a work of art, preferably one listed in their role sheets, but other works may be substituted and discussed, as long as they were not produced after 1889. Artists should not limit themselves to just one work; one is the minimum. Furthermore, they should talk about their ideas about art rather than simply describe the paintings. They must explain what they are attempting to express in their work and why it is superb. Every role sheet lists multiple examples of appropriate work.

Critics

Critics use their speeches to bestow Critic Tickets on the artists of their choice. The Critic Tickets are highly prized because they give the recipient an automatic sale in 1889. If that artist shows with others, the possession of the Critic Ticket also guarantees another sale to someone in that show— that artist or a fellow artist (decided by die rolls).

The Critic Ticket speech **must** discuss works of art by the artist on whom the ticket is being bestowed. But the speech must not simply describe the works of art. Instead, critics must explain to the assembled audience **what** the ticketed artist is attempting to express in his or her work and **why** that work is better than the work of others. Critic Tickets are attached to the critic role sheets and are authenticated by the GM.

Dealers

Dealers must advertise. Dealers care about sales. They know that the art-buying public is fickle but tends to trust dealers who consistently express their knowledge of the art world and show an appreciation for what is going on. Dealers demonstrate their knowledge by creating broadsides that promote their galleries and describe works of art that they have exhibited in the past. This may require the dealer to do some research on the art market in nineteenth-century Paris. For the game, all dealers must create and circulate ideas in the form of broadsides for at least sessions 2 and 3.

For Game Session 4, dealers must announce in a formal speech the works that they will display at the 1889 Exposition Universelle. The speech must name the works and describe and discuss them in detail. Dealers must explain **why** they chose the particular artist or artists and **why** the work is better than the work of others.

COUNTERFACTUALS

The artists, critics, and dealers in this game were all active participants in the Paris art scene during this era, but they likely never all collected together in a single room. However, *anyone*—artist, critic, and dealer alike—would have visited the annual Paris Salon, sponsored by the Academy.

4

Roles and Factions

These are short profiles for all characters in the game. The factions listed here are more of a quick reference guide than a set of hard and fast alliances. Many of these figures moved between these groups over time. For example, some of the artists listed in categories other than "Impressionist" affiliated with this group in the past (for instance, Cézanne exhibited in the first Impressionist exhibition). In addition, different cross-references might result in different factions.

The works listed are representative of the artist's style and should be considered important textual information on the artist and his or her aesthetic considerations. Images should be searched for on an Internet search engine.

ACADEMY MEMBERS

William-Adolphe Bouguereau is a very distinguished and important academic painter. He was elected a lifetime member of the Academy in 1876. He is the president of the Salon in 1888 and will lead the first session's debates. Works that represent his style include *Nymphs and Satyrs* (1873) and *The Birth of Venus* (1879). More recent work includes *Rite of Spring* (1886).

Jean-Louis Ernest Meissonier is a very distinguished and important academic painter. He was elected a lifetime member of the Academy in 1861. Works that represent his style include *Friedland, 1807* (1861–75), *Campagne de France, 1814 (Napoléon Returning from Russia)* (1864), and *The Siege of Paris* (1884).

Jean-Léon Gérôme is a very distinguished and important academic painter. He was elected a lifetime member of the Academy in 1865. Works that represent his style include *The Snake Charmer* (ca. 1870), *The Roman Slave* (1884), and *The Carpet Merchant* (1887).

Jules Adolphe Aimé Louis Breton favors paintings of peasants in the rural French landscape, such as *The Song of the Lark* (1884). He was elected a lifetime member of the Academy in 1886. His painting *Young Women Going to a Procession* was shown in the 1888 Salon.

PROMINENT ARTISTS

Pierre Auguste Renoir is a painter who has shown with the Impressionists but has also submitted works to the annual Salons. Works that represent his style include *Dance at the Moulin de la Galette* (1876), *Madame Charpentier and Her Daughters* (1878), and, more recently, *The Great Bathers* (1884–87).

Pierre Puvis de Chavannes is an artist who is often commissioned to paint for government buildings. He is a juror for some of the medals in the 1888 Salon. His paintings of the life of Saint Geneviève are on view in the Panthéon in Paris and were painted in 1877. Other works that represent his style include *Hope* (1872), *The Poor Fisherman* (1881), and *Sacred Wood Dear to the Arts and Muses* (1884).

Gustave Moreau is an artist interested in mythological subjects. His first important work accepted to the Salon was *Oedipus and the Sphinx* (1864). Other works that are representative of his style include *Prometheus* (1868), *The Apparition* (1874), and *Jupiter and Semele* (1875). This year, 1888, he painted *The Victorious Sphinx*.

IMPRESSIONISTS

Claude Monet focuses much of his painting on landscapes. He paints outdoors, preferring to travel to the outskirts of Paris by train in order to paint. His style is best represented by the following works: *On the Banks of the Seine* (1868), *Le Pont de l'Europe, Gare Saint-Lazare* (1877), and the painting that gave its name to the movement, *Impression, Sunrise* (1872).

Edgar Degas is very much interested in recording the everyday people of France in order to represent the new "modern" city. He tends to think of the annual Salon as tired and worn, with nothing new to offer. He has no interest in ever showing at the Salon. His style is represented by *The Place de la Concorde (Viscount Lepic and His Daughters)* (1873), *The Absinthe Drinker* (1876), his numerous portrayals of the ballet and various dancers, and his pastel series—most recently, his

series of women bathing, most notably *The Tub* (1886).

Berthe Morisot is one of the founding members of the Impressionist movement, missing only one of its eight exhibitions—the one in 1879, after giving birth. Morisot was very close to Édouard Manet and married his brother in 1874. She greatly influenced the work of Manet and other painters. Her style is best represented by the following paintings: *The Cradle* (1872), *On the Balcony* (1872), and *Woman at Her Toilette* (1875).

NEO-IMPRESSIONISTS

Camille Pissarro has embraced many styles. A landscape painter in the 1850s and 1860s, Pissarro also embraced the Impressionist movement and was one of the principal organizers of the first show. He is now intrigued by Neo-Impressionism, a style that is being produced by artists such as Seurat and Signac. Examples of his work include *Hoar Frost* (1873), *The Old Road to Ennery, Pontoise* (1877), *Shepherdess (Young Peasant Girl with a Stick)* (1881), and *Apple Picking at Éragny-sur-Epte* (1888).

Georges Seurat is very interested in the scientific properties of color that have been recently published and discussed. He has devised a painting system based on these color theories, which some call Neo-Impressionism. Some of his representative works include *Bathers at Asnières* (1883–84), *Sunday Afternoon on the Island of La Grande Jatte* (1884–86), and, most recently *Circus Sideshow* (1887–88).

Paul Signac has recently embraced the Neo-Impressionist techniques of Seurat. He, too, is interested in new color theories and discussions. Paintings that represent his style include *The Seine at Asnières* (1885), *The River Bank, Petit-Andely* (1886), and *The Dining Room* (1886–87).

AVANT-GARDE ARTISTS

Paul Cézanne has shown some works with the Impressionists at their group shows. Some of his works with the Impressionists include *A Modern Olympia* (1873–74) and *The Hanged Man's House*

(1874). More recent work by Cézanne includes his many views of Mont Sainte-Victoire (1882–87) and *The Great Bather* (1885).

Vincent Van Gogh is an artist originally from Holland. He has not been in Paris long and has not been painting for long, either. He paints people in his life, including his landlady in Arles, *L'Arlésienne (Mme. Ginoux)* (1888), and *Père Tanguy* (1887). He is also drawn to depicting flowers and landscapes, such as his painting *Starry Night* (1888). He also painted *The Night Café* (1888).

Paul Gauguin is a banker turned artist. He is very much interested in what the arts of the primitive cultures can bring to the modern European art world. He is especially interested in the art of Africa and Asia. He has often stated his desire to express the spiritual in art, which is best exemplified in his *Vision after the Sermon* (1888). Other paintings from this year include *Still Life with Three Puppies* (1888) and *Breton Women in a Meadow* (1888).

Henri de Toulouse-Lautrec is an aristocrat by birth. However, he suffered major maladies in childhood that have left him deformed. In spite of his odd appearance, Toulouse-Lautrec does not hide from the public and spends much of his time in the artists' haven of Montmartre in Paris. His works at this time include *The Laundress* (1884–88), *Adéle de Toulouse-Lautrec in the Salon at Malromé* (1886), and *At the Circus Fernando* (1888). This last work is the most representative of his current style.

AMERICAN ARTISTS

Mary Cassatt is an American artist who has shown with the Impressionists. She has also submitted some works to the annual Salons and has met with modest but not exceptional success. She is very much an admirer of Edgar Degas. Good representations of her work include *In the Loge* (1876), *Portrait of the Artist* (1878), and a pastel of her sister, Lydia, titled *Lydia Leaning on Her Arms, Seated in Loge* (1879).

John Singer Sargent is an artist from America most known for his portraits. He has had success in various Paris Salons, and his portrait of *Mme. Playfair* was accepted in the 1888 Salon. His most notorious painting is of *Mme. Pierre Gautreau* (also known as *Madame X*), which caused quite a scandal in the Parisian art world when it was painted in 1883. He has had some connections with the Impressionists as well.

James McNeil Whistler is an American artist who has spent a lot of time in England but has also had some success in Paris. He had submitted the infamous *Symphony in White, No. 1: The White Girl* to the Salon of 1863, but it was rejected and shown in the Salon des Refusés instead that same year. He has painted portraits, but is also known for his paintings called nocturnes. He had a tussle with the art critic John Ruskin, whom the artist sued for libel and won. In addition to *The White Girl*, important works include *At the Piano* (1858–59), *Nocturne: Blue and Gold—Old Battersea Bridge* (1872–77), and *Nocturne in Black and Gold: The Falling Rocket* (1875).

CRITICS

Joséphin Péladan is very much interested in the ideal, in tradition, and in hierarchy. He tends to advocate conservatism in art. He is a devout Catholic.

Joris-Karl Huysmans has written quite a bit about Impressionism, noting that it is an important movement. He likes the emphasis on the middle class that these artists embrace. He is more recently drawn to artists he considers able to represent a certain decadence seen in modern times.

Félix Fénéon quickly became familiar with the Impressionists, who began showing when he was only in his teens. He now wants to see art move beyond Impressionism into what he terms "Neo-Impressionism" and seeks artists that match his ideas on this new style. He also praises art that embraces the hieratic and the traditional. There have also been rumors that he has connections with anarchists.

G.-Albert Aurier invented the term "ideaist" to contrast with the Academy's concept of the "ideal."

He promotes art that is based on ideas, not on mundane facts. He is also a proponent of the decorative in art, and speaks favorably about the art of the Renaissance masters. He is not a fan of the Salons and seeks something new.

André Michel is rather conservative in his thinking. He is concerned that painting has become a slave to the public, eschewing high ideals for sentimental entertainment that titillates rather than inspires the public.

DEALERS

Paul Durand-Ruel is an art dealer in Paris. His chief rival is Georges Petit.

Georges Petit is an art dealer in Paris. His chief rival is Paul Durand-Ruel.

5

Core Texts and Documents

You may wish to examine works of art by different artists on your computer or another electronic device as you read.

The following four paintings were completed in 1888 and are essential to the game. Your professor may make them available to you via a course management system; otherwise, look them up on your computer through an Internet search. You will need to examine them closely and critically. Read through Appendix A on formal analysis, and use the terms discussed in your examination of these four images:

Édouard Detaille's *The Dream*. 1888. Musée d'Orsay, Paris.

Pierre Puvis de Chavannes, *Between Art and Nature*. 1888. Metropolitan Museum of Art, New York City.

Claude Monet, *Morning at Antibes*. 1888. Now in Philadelphia Museum of Art, Pennsylvania.

Paul Gauguin, *Still Life with Three Puppies*. 1888. Now in the Museum of Modern Art, New York City.

WRITTEN DOCUMENTS

The following are important works written by art critics central to the game. Everyone should read these examples of art criticism (not just those in the roles of the critics who wrote them). When possible, these texts should be referenced in speeches by artists, critics, and dealers. Although these critics do not reference every artist in the game, general ideas about art and the future of art can be understood once these texts are examined critically and read carefully.

Additional written art criticism is available from the GM. It includes:

G.-Albert Aurier, "Essay on a New Method of Criticism" and "Symbolism in Painting: Paul Gauguin," both in Herschel B. Chipp, *Theories of Modern Art* (Berkeley: University of California Press, 1968), 87–93.

Joséphin Péladan, "Materialism in Art" and "In Search of the Holy Grail," both in Henri Dorra, *Symbolist Art Theories: A Critical Anthology* (Berkeley: University of California Press, 1994), 264–69.

Félix Fénéon, "On the Third Exhibition of the Société des Artistes Indépendants," also in Henri Dorra, *Symbolist Art Theories: A Critical Anthology* (Berkeley: University of California Press, 1994), 160–63.

Joris-Karl Huysmans

Like Emile Zola and other authors associated with the naturalist movement in literature, J-K Huysmans supported the Impressionists for portraying the everyday subjects they all favored. Huysmans was particularly close to Degas and wrote extensively about the artist, praising his innovative ability to capture precisely the actions and gestures that define human character. Huysmans would later abandon naturalism and become the dominant figure of the decadent movement in literature. In doing so, he became the main champion of Gustave Moreau, seeing in Moreau the same isolation and solitary genius he saw in Degas.

"The Exposition of Indépendants in 1880"
Source: "L'Exposition des Indépendants en 1880," in L'Art Moderne *(Paris: Charpentiere, 1883), 135–36. Translation by Michael A. Marlais, 2009.*

When will this painter [Degas] be assigned the high place that is his due in the world of art? When will it be understood that this artist is the greatest we possess today in France? I am not a prophet, but if I am to judge by the ineptitude of the enlightened classes, who despised Delacroix for so long; who have still not the least suspicion that Baudelaire is the poetic genius of the nineteenth century, dwarfing every other poet including Hugo; or that the masterpiece of the modern novel is Gustave Flaubert's *L'Education sentimentale*—and with literature being the so-called most accessible art to the masses!—I can believe the truth of what I am the only one to write today, that M. Degas will probably not be recognized for a long, long time.

On Degas, 1889
Source: From Certains *(Paris: Tresse & Stock, 1889), 27. Translation by Michael A. Marlais, 2009.*

A powerful and isolated artist, with no known precedent, without validating lineage, M. Degas creates in each of his canvases the sensation of the oddly precise, the thing so right that one is surprised to be astonished, that one almost wishes it; his work belongs to realism, such as that brute Courbet could never understand, but that is reminiscent of some of the Primitives, that is to say of an art expressing an expansive uplifting, or the essence of a soul, in the living bodies, in perfect harmony with their surroundings.

"The Exposition of Indépendants in 1881"
Source: "L'Exposition des Indépendants en 1881," in L'Art Moderne *(Paris: Charpentiere, 1883), 279–82. Translation by Michael A. Marlais, 2009.*

The exposition of the Independents will be important this time, it is the revelation, already begun, of a new art, and it seems to be an irrefutable argument to the still unresolved question of the relationships between the State and Art. Noting how the state, in response to complaints from the artists, had withdrawn support of the Salon the previous year and allowed the artists to choose new juries, or no juries at all, no prizes, in essence, something seemingly new. Then, like tamed beasts, the painters refused to rouse themselves, to free themselves, and they went back post-haste to their stables, declaring that all was better in the stud farm, and that they wanted finally to keep . . . their old masters.

Consequently Bonnat, Cabanel, Laurens, all the old teachers, were re-elected members of the jury [for the annual Salon], and by vote of the people who had for so long demanded that they be shelved; nothing has changed, these are the same men who accepted or rejected canvases, who supported their own students. This is what all the liberal intentions have resulted in. To tell the truth, the state made a false move. It had wanted to run with the hare and hunt with the hound, to continue, in spite of the appearance of disinterest, to patronize and to give prizes to painters, rather than have them go on to other venues, and let them shift for themselves, to open if they wanted, some galleries and distribute prospectuses.

There is no more any reason, in effect, to protect and medal painters than there is to aid and decorate writers and musicians. Those who have personality will end by breaking through perhaps and, the remainder, their type remains the same, whether they eliminate or keep the medals and the official titles, since they are assured to never have any. As to the others, they will become employees in business if they get the instruction, peddlers or street sweepers if they don't know how to count or read. At any rate, this type does not bother me, they will continue to daub at painting, because the less one has talent the more one has the chance to make a living in art!

"On Dilettantism," 1889
Source: "Du Dilettantisme," in Certains *(Paris: Tresse & Stock, 1889), 7–13. Translation by Michael A. Marlais, 2009.*

One of the most disconcerting symptoms of this époque is promiscuity in admiration. Art having become, like sport, one of the sought after hobbies of rich people, exhibitions are followed with equal success, whatever the works on exhibit, provided that the merchants of the press get involved and that the display takes place in a known gallery, in a hall reputed in good form by all.

The vogue for these diversions is self-explanatory.

First, the arid minds of men of the world discover in the regular side show of drawings and canvases frivolous resources that can alternate with tired discussions of politics and the boring din on the theatre; then the common places about painting sometimes also supply, in the evening, worldly gossip, and stir the somnambulant thoughts or the diplomatic silences of whist players.

Finally,—and this reason suffices by itself—to visit and, so to speak, admire works of art that are the most different and the most hostile to each other, implies a largeness of spirit, an elasticity of artistic pleasure, that is truly flattering. . . .

Cowardice, that's the word that describes art criticism these days. Just like the literary critic who has become a careerist the art critic is generally a man of letters who has not been able to produce on his own a true work of art. Among them, some of the vacuity of mind of the men of the world that they envy and imitate. Their opinions are commonplace. But there are others, more open, more cunning, who profess, under the name of dilettantism, the necessity to not take sides, the need to affirm nothing, the cowardice, to say it correctly, of thought and the hypocrisy of form. . . .

No, the truth is that one cannot understand art and truly love it if one is an eclectic, a dilettante. One cannot sincerely go into ecstasies over Delacrox if one admires M. Bastien-Lepage; one does not like M. Gustave Moreau if one accepts M. Bonnat, nor M. Degas if one tolerates M. Gervex.

Fortunately the profitable estate of the dilettante has its drawbacks: in these excesses of pusillanimity, these debauches of prudence, language inevitably grows feeble and fluid, reverts to the dreary, murky style of the Institutes, liquefies into the damp diction of M. Renan. For one cannot have talent unless one loves with passion and hates with passion, enthusiasm and contempt are indispensable for creating a work of art, talent goes to the sincere and the fanatical, not to the indifferent and fearful.

And how many painters are there now who paint and who rage and suffer for their works?

"Gustave Moreau," 1889
Source: "Gustave Moreau," in Certains *(Paris: Tresse & Stock, 1889), 17–20. Translation by Michael A. Marlais, 2009.*

Away from the maddening crowd [of Salon artists], which provides us during the month of Mary [May] with intellectual ipecac of great art, Gustave Moreau for years has kept his canvases from becoming prisoners under the drab muslin tents hanging like miserable canopies in the glassed-in structure of the Palace of Industry.

He has also abstained from showing them in fashionable society exhibitions. As a result, his works, held by a few dealers, are rarely seen. In 1886, however, a series of his watercolors was exhibited by the Goupils in their galleries, rue Chaptal.

There the rooms were filled with immense skies lit by the flames of an auto-da-fé; squashed globes of bleeding suns, hemorrhages of heavenly bodies poured down in purple cataracts over scudding clouds.

Against the terrible bustle of such backgrounds, silent women went by, naked or dressed in gowns adorned with precious stones, like old Gospel-book bindings; women with hair of raw silk; with hard, steady gazes darting from pale blue eyes; with flesh as white and icy as the seminal fluid of fish; motionless Salomes holding in a cup the glowing head of the Precursor [Saint John the Baptist], macerated in phosphorus, under topiaries with twisted branches of green verging on black; goddesses riding hippogriffs and slicing with the lapis of their wings the swarms of agonizing clouds; feminine idols wearing tiaras, standing on thrones whose steps are awash in extraordinary flowers or else seated, in rigid poses, on elephants whose foreheads are weighted with green decorations, whose chests are cloaked in gold-embroidered chasubles, edged with pearls in the guise of jingle bells, elephants who stamp on their weighty image, reflected in the surface of the water they splash with their columnar ring-encircled legs.

An identical impression arose from these various scenes, an impression of repeated spiritual onanism in a chaste flesh; the impression of a virgin endowed with a solemnly graceful body, with a soul exhausted by solitary secret thoughts; of a woman seated, murmuring to herself, under the pretense of the sacramental rhetoric of obscure prayers, insidious appeals for sacrilege, shameful orgies, torture, and murder.

Out of that gallery, in the bleak street, the dazed memory of these works persisted, but the scenes no longer appeared in their entirety; they became unremittingly fragmented into the minutiae of their strange details. The execution of these jewels, their outlines incised in the watercolor as if with the squashed nibs of pens; the thin elegance of these plants with intertwining stalks; the partially interwoven stems, embroidered like the lace surplices once made for prelates; the sweep of these flowers pertaining through their shape both to religious vessels and to aquatic flora, to water lilies and *pyxides*, chalices and algae, all this surprising chemistry of shrill colors, which, having reached their ultimate stage, went to the head and intoxicated the sight, causing the departing visitor, totally blinded by what he still saw projected along the new houses [lining the street] to grope for his way.

On second thought, as I went on strolling, as my eye found a new serenity and could look at, and size up, the shame of modern taste, the street— these boulevards where trees that have been orthopedically corseted in iron and fitted by the trussers of the Department of Public Works in cast-iron wheels [railings and circular grates placed around trees in Paris to protect them]; these roadways shaken by enormous horse-drawn buses and ignoble publicity carts; these sidewalks filled with a hideous crowd in quest of money: with women degraded by successive confinements, made stupid by horrible barters; with men reading vile newspapers or dreaming of fornications or of fraudulent operations [as they walked] along the shops and offices from which the officially sanctioned crooks of business and finance spy, the better to prey on them—one understood better the work of Gustave Moreau, which stands outside time, escapes into distant realms, glides over dreams, away from the excremental ideas oozing from a whole populace.

G.-Albert Aurier

G.-Albert Aurier, who would become the first critic to write articles about both Paul Gauguin and Vincent van Gogh, was a skillful art critic. Indeed, his art criticism has far outlasted his literary efforts. He wrote stinging criticism of academic art and the standard fare produced year after year at the annual Paris Salons. For all the differences of the circles in which they operated, he shared a passion for the ideal that permeated the criticism of Joséphin Péladan. They were both adept at intellectually trashing art they did not admire.

"The Salon of 1888"

Source: "Le Salon de 1888," Le Décadent, May 15–31, 1888, 9. Translated by Michael A. Marlais, 2009.

The exhibition this year scarcely merits serious treatment. If the word "mediocre" did not exist, it would indeed have to be invented to characterize it. And if there were degrees of mediocrity, I would willfully place this exhibition well beneath its mediocre cousins.—General impression: dreadful insignificance, nauseating platitude, not a single stroke of genius to strike you, scarcely twenty good things, as always a jumble of foolishness, of twaddle, of pastiches, ineptitudes, of facile but impersonal charlantry which comes from every salon, witness that *good pupils* are not lacking in France, and consequently, daubs, daubs, shameless daubs, innumerable daubs. I looked everywhere, from floor to ceiling, searching for something new, original, personal, a tentative emancipation, a minute something that hasn't already been seen—Nothing! Nothing! These poor workers move around in the same circle, in the same merry-go-round, on their same eternal wooden horses.

Joséphin Péladan

Joséphin Péladan was an unabashed ultraconservative Catholic and monarchist at a time when most Parisian intellectuals were republican and not religious. He longed for a return to the great religious art of the

Italian Renaissance and hated any art that dealt with realist subjects. He was a dramatic and effective art critic, making grand proclamations that grabbed attention. He would become a steadfast advocate of the art of Puvis de Chavannes.

"The Aesthetics at the Salon of 1883"

Source: "L'Esthetique au Salon de 1883," in L'Art Ochlocratique (Paris: Camille Dalou, 1888). Excerpts translated by Michael A. Marlais, 2009.

I believe in the Ideal, in Tradition, in Hierarchy. That is the text of this aesthetic homily.

The critic is a judge who must announce the law, before applying it, above all in a period when they debate the process of art without rules, according to the mood of the day, the needs of colleagues, and galleries. . . .

The Salon is always the bazaar, sometimes the bedroom, never the temple of painting; a Pnyx, not an Acropolis, and not at all a painting museum. The first May of every year, four thousand works appear . . . and in this heap two thousand manufactured items, a thousand products, and works of art. . . .

Painting, sculpture, architecture have become businesses; and among four thousands artist, there are three thousand artisans, falsely proud, fiercely bull-headed. The disdain that is due to them should not be held back. . . .

Before searching for the nature of contemporary art, it is opportune to note contemporary aesthetic opinion. There are eclectic art critics, eclecticism being the absence of opinion. There are the opinions of amateurs who would sell an authentic Botticelli at auction for twelve hundred francs and then pay fifteen hundred francs for a Boucher. There are the opinions of the bourgeoisie who love trite genre paintings and military subjects. There are opinions of those who love the touch of paint, who praise only facile paint handling.

The history of art and its hierarchy are poorly known, if not disregarded, and the lack of respect of the masters of the past has no limits. . . .

We are clearly in a period of eclecticism, none can contest that. But eclecticism is the absence of passion, and without passion there is no longer poetry in art. . . . Where are the artists who love painting, and who paint for the joy of painting? Thus, no enthusiasm, and here I would touch on one of the causes of the decline of painting; it is the artists' ignorance, their lack of instruction and of reading. They no longer seek to penetrate the spirit of their subjects, so when they take a scene from Homer or Dante, they don't read in front of their canvases, before drawing the Iliad or the Divine Comedy. . . .

I have the naiveté to believe that to paint a Christ, for example, one must re-read each day the story of the passion and feel what one paints, while painting, and if not one is just doing business. . . .

Art is the effort of humans to realize the Ideal, to embody and represent the supreme idea, the idea par excellence, the abstract idea, and the grand masterpieces of art are religious, because to materialize the idea of God, the idea of an angel, the idea of the Virgin Mother, demands an incomparable effort of thought and technique. To render the invisible visible, there is the true goal of art and its only reason to exist. . . . If the ideal is the necessity of grand art, tradition is its law. They link between them, by the golden chain of masterpieces, universal concepts. That is the esthetic dogma, the great works are bibles. The first rule of tradition is that art must be a synthesis. . . . Because synthesis only is concerned with the transfiguration of the human being, whether obtained by the purity of form of the Italians, the light of Rembrandt, by the lively accent as in Rubens and Velasquez. . . . Art gives the lie to reality. . . . It must always be more beautiful, or more ugly, than the real. . . .

But grand art is finished, irremediably finished. . . . The ideal is dead, tradition is dead, hierarchy is dead. . . .

To those who find this lamentation naïve and distressing I would say: Hold at the thought of the art of the past, the grand art of the past, in comparison with what is left to us now, and you judge what we have remaining today.

Here is the epitaph of the Salon of 1883: DECADENCE!

André Michel

An art historian educated at the École practique des hautes études under famed historian Hippolyte Taine, Michel was very much part of the intellectual establishment. In 1888 he was teaching art history at a prestigious private school of architecture in Paris. Like many intellectuals of the period, he also wrote reviews of the annual Salons, publishing in some of the most important journals of the day. He would go on to write several books about the history of modern art. Early on he became devoted to the work of Puvis de Chavannes and wrote eloquently of the artist's ability, indeed duty, to synthesize nature, to simplify and change pictorial reality according to his individual temperament. He was also a fierce critic of what he saw as the degraded tastes of the typical Salon audience.

"The Salon of 1884"

Source: "Le Salon de 1884," L'Art 36 (1884): 161–67. Translation by Michael A. Marlais, 1992.

The greater part (of the Salon audience) only sees the subject of a painting, interesting or boring, pleasing or sad, and they get the same pleasure there as from a vaudeville entertainment or a sentimental romance. A whole class of painters— those that are called *genre*—have found in this taste a great outlet and disastrous encouragement. It is necessary, in effect, for a busy and superficial society to have an art easy to house and easy to understand because apartments are small and business absorbing. . . . Amusing and decorative painting are very much on the march and one could say that it is the least artistic part of the public that exercises the most considerable influence on artistic production.

"Puvis de Chavannes Exhibition"

Source: "Exposition de M. Puvis de Chavannes," Gazette des Beaux-Arts 36 (January 1888): 36–44. *Translation by Michael A. Marlais, 2017.*

There has been with M. Puvis de Chavannes a perfect accord, more rare than one thinks, between native aptitude and the form of art that he has dedicated himself to. . . . He was marvelously prepared to formulate grand plastic expressions which demand summary and synthetic silhouettes, simple lines, disciplined and combined in composed ensembles, where large contrasting tonalities vibrate in silence, like an enveloping and distant andante of sweet harmony.

Supplemental Documents

PRIMARY SOURCES

Much of the art criticism in the gamebook was drawn from the following two sources:

Chipp, Herschel B. *Theories of Modern Art.* Berkeley: University of California Press, 1968.

Dorra, Henri. *Symbolist Art Theories: A Critical Anthology.* Berkeley: University of California Press, 1994.

These texts feature pieces of art criticism that are not included in this gamebook. Consequently, it can be useful to place these on reserve in a library. These include:

Aurier, G.-Albert. "The Lonely Ones—Vincent van Gogh (1890)." In Dorra, *Symbolist Art Theories*, 218–26.

———. "The Symbolist Painters." In Chipp, *Theories of Modern Art*, 93–94.

Huysmans, Joris-Karl. "Cézanne (1888)." In Dorra, *Symbolist Art Theories*, 227–29.

SECONDARY SOURCES ON ART CRITICISM

Baldick, Robert. *The Life of J.-K. Huysmans.* Sawtry, Cambridgeshire: Dedalus, 2006. First published in 1955 but still the major work on Huysmans.

Brookner, Anita. "Huysmans." In *The Genius of the Future: Studies in French Art Criticism*, 147–67. New York: Phaidon, 1971.

———. "Huysmans: The Madness of Art." In *Romanticism and Its Discontents*, 161–81. New York: Farrar, Straus and Giroux, 2000.

Halperin, Joan Ungersma. *Félix Fénéon: Aesthete and Anarchist in Fin-de-siècle Paris.* New Haven, CT: Yale University Press, 1988.

Mathews, Patricia Townley. *Aurier's Symbolist Art Criticism and Theory.* Ann Arbor, MI: UMI Research Press, 1986.

Rewald, John. "Felix Fénéon." *Gazette des Beaux-Arts*, July–August 1947, 45–62; February 1948, 107–26.

Acknowledgments

We greatly appreciate the encouragement we have received from the Reacting Consortium.

Playtesting is key to developing any game. We've benefited from numerous enthusiastic and supportive playtesters, but a few have been key in helping us refine the game. These playtesters include Mary Beth Looney, Molly McClain, Margaret Morse, Terri Nelson, and Elissa Auerbach.

Emily Machen provided cogent advice on background readings in the cultural history of nineteenth-century France.

Mary Jane Treacy eagerly took on the job of development editor for the game in 2012. Her detailed feedback has been instrumental in shaping and improving the game.

David Henderson and Paula Lazrus also offered excellent advice as readers.

Appendix A. How to Read a Visual Image

A PRIMER ON FORMAL ELEMENTS

In the same way that people discuss books and films, images can be examined and understood. Becoming familiar with and understanding the terminology that art historians use is the first step to feeling comfortable talking about a painting—and you will need to be familiar with how to analyze paintings for our game. To be able to talk about an image, you need to first understand its **formal qualities**, which are discussed in this section.

The most important thing you must do when setting out to talk about an image is to **look at it**—but not in a cursory way. To begin to gauge a painting's potential meaning, significance, or even importance, you must examine it carefully, noting elements of its formal construction. The qualities you will need to consider are as follows:

Style: A style is created when certain formal elements are shared among works of art from a particular period. For instance, there will be some formal similarities for all paintings considered Impressionism, which is a type of *style*.

Subject: Except for some examples in modern art, which follows on the heels of the art of our game, art has a subject. You need to be able to discern the subject of your work in order to examine the way the artist goes about painting it. Examining how the subject is portrayed is often the first step in assigning a meaning to that image.

Material: This refers to the physical objects required to make the image. For this game, most paintings are oil paintings on canvas. However, artists used different types of materials in painting through history. For instance, during the Renaissance, frescoes (which Puvis de Chavannes attempts to emulate in oil painting) were painted on wet plaster so that the finished work literally adhered to the wall's surface.

Line: This refers to the movement of your eyes as you look at a work of art. Horizontal and vertical lines in a composition create an image that is balanced and solid. Diagonal lines add movement and action because your eyes will dart along a diagonal. Circular lines move your eyes around a composition.

Color: The way that color is applied to the canvas affects many things: the way a viewer encounters it, the meaning of the piece, and a viewer's experience of the work. Color can be very bright or more subdued; this refers to its value. Primary colors are blue, yellow, and red; they cannot be created by mixing other colors. Complementary colors are opposites on a color wheel; they create a jarring effect when placed next to each other (purple–yellow, orange–blue, red–green). Colors can be of lighter saturation (like paintings by Morisot) or very highly saturated and bright (like the work of Van Gogh).

Texture: The way that paint is applied and experienced is also an important element of art. Van Gogh applies paint with a heavy hand; you can actually see the imprint of his palette knife and brushes in the finished painting, and you can see how he applied the paint. Cézanne incorporates a lot of texture in his work, as do the Impressionists. Only the traditional academic painters believed that the "hand of the artist" should never be seen. This is an important distinction in the works of art in our game.

Space (mass, volume): A painting can seem to take up a lot of space, or it can seem flat. A painting *is* flat; it is a two-dimensional object. However, artists can create the illusion of space using perspective (see next entry). If perspective is used, then the objects in the painting will appear to be real and create a sense of three-dimensional space. Remember, however, that although artists can trick a viewer into seeing three dimensions, a painting is only ever a two-dimensional surface. In our game, some artists—especially Cézanne and some of the other avant-garde artists—began to struggle with this dichotomy, feeling that this "trickery" constituted lying to the public. Other artists in the game believe that the ability to transform a flat surface into a three-dimensional scene is a wonder and the true craft of an artist.

Perspective: To achieve a look of three-dimensionality in a painting, an artist often employs one-point linear perspective. In this system, a vanishing point is chosen somewhere in the background of the canvas, and all lines recede to this point. These lines are called "orthogonals." Sometimes artists also employ foreshortening to make things that appear in the foreground recede to a sense of "normal" space. Some artists feel that these techniques constitute trickery and want to bring a sense

of truthfulness to art. Other artists feel that mirroring nature destroys the spirituality of art and thus seek a different way of expressing space and spurn perspectival practices in their paintings. Another form of perspective is "atmospheric perspective." This is a way of painting by which objects that are farther away in the painting are blurrier than those that are in the foreground.

Proportion: To make a work of art seem true to natural forms, all elements in the painting should be balanced and replicate proportions that exist in nature. This means that if painting a person, the head and body will be measured in relation to each other. Ideal proportions for the human body change over time in sculpture (e.g., the Greeks had a very different sense of proportion than did the ancient Egyptians). In painting, artists sometimes exaggerate proportions on an individual to make some sort of declaration about that person. Some of the portraits by Van Gogh exaggerate certain features to highlight them in some way. When an artist deviates from "natural" proportions, this is a tip that the artist is trying to make some sort of statement, and it is up to the viewer to attempt to interpret it.

Appendix B. Seats of the Academy in 1888

The following list shows the artists who held the fourteen seats in the Academy in 1888.

Gustave Boulanger, the occupant of seat 9, died in 1888, leaving this seat open for a new artist to join the ranks.

Seat 1: Emile Signol, elected 1860.
Seat 2: Louis Cabat, elected 1867.
Seat 3: Jean-Léon Gérôme, elected 1865.
Seat 4: Joseph-Nicolas Robert-Fleury, elected 1850.

Seat 5: Jules Delaunay, elected 1879.
Seat 6: Charles-Louis Müller, elected 1864.
Seat 7: Léon Bonnat, elected 1881.
Seat 8: Jules Breton, elected 1886.
Seat 9: Gustave Boulanger, elected 1882.
Seat 10: Alexandre Cabanel, elected 1863.
Seat 11: Antoine Hébert, elected 1874.
Seat 12: Jean Meissonier, elected 1861.
Seat 13: Jules Lenepveu, elected 1869.
Seat 14: William Bouguereau, elected 1876.

www.ingramcontent.com/pod-product-compliance
Lightning Source LLC
Chambersburg PA
CBHW081313170526
45166CB00011B/3515